THE
GUIDE TO
NATIONAL
PARKS
OF THE
SOUTHWEST

WRITTEN BY

NICKY J. LEACH

PHOTOGRAPHY BY

GEORGE H. H. HUEY

SOUTHWEST PARKS & MONUMENTS ASSOCIATION
TUCSON, ARIZONA

Copyright © 1992 by Southwest Parks & Monuments
Association, Tucson, Arizona 85701
www.spma.org

ISBN 1-877856-14-2

Library of Congress Number 91-68245

Fourth printing: revised and updated, January 1999.

Produced for Southwest Parks & Monuments Association by
LATRANS BOOKS, Prescott, Arizona.

Book design: Christina Watkins.
Editor: Rose Houk.
Editorial assistance: Randolph Jorgen, Ron Foreman,
and T. J. Priehs.
Typography: TypeWorks, Tucson, Arizona.
Lithography: Lorraine Press, Salt Lake City, Utah.
Maps: Deborah Reade.

All photographs copyright George H. H. Huey, unless otherwise
credited.

Cover photograph: Cactus forest, Saguaro National Park,
Arizona.

Cover rug details: Navajo rug E3176, Courtesy The Museum
of Northern Arizona.

Frontispiece: Eagle claw cactus, Big Bend National Park,
Texas.

♻ Printed on recycled paper with vegetable-based inks.

CONTENTS

Map of the Southwest 5

ARCHES National Park 6

AZTEC RUINS National Monument 8

BANDELIER National Monument 9

BENT'S OLD FORT National Historic Site 11

BIG BEND National Park 12

BLACK CANYON OF THE GUNNISON National Monument 14

BRYCE CANYON National Park 15

CANYON de CHELLY National Monument 17

CANYONLANDS National Park 19

CAPITOL REEF National Park 22

CAPULIN VOLCANO National Monument 24

CARLSBAD CAVERNS National Park 25

CASA GRANDE RUINS National Monument 27

CEDAR BREAKS National Monument 28

CHACO CULTURE National Historical Park 29

CHAMIZAL National Memorial 31

CHIRICAHUA National Monument 32

CORONADO National Memorial 33

CURECANTI National Recreation Area 34

EL MALPAIS National Monument 35

EL MORRO National Monument 36

FORT BOWIE National Historic Site 37

FORT DAVIS National Historic Site 38

FORT UNION National Monument 39

GILA CLIFF DWELLINGS National Monument 40

GLEN CANYON National Recreational Area 41

GRAND CANYON National Park 43

GREAT SAND DUNES National Monument 46

GUADALUPE MOUNTAINS National Park 47

HOVENWEEP National Monument 49

HUBBELL TRADING POST National Historic Site 50

LAKE MEAD National Recreational Area 51

MESA VERDE National Park 53

MONTEZUMA CASTLE National Monument 55

NATURAL BRIDGES National Monument 56

NAVAJO National Monument 57

ORGAN PIPE CACTUS National Monument 58

PECOS National Historical Park 60

PETRIFIED FOREST National Park 61

PETROGLYPH National Monument 63

PIPE SPRING National Monument 64

RAINBOW BRIDGE National Monument 65

SAGUARO National Park 66

SALINAS PUEBLO MISSIONS National Monument 68

SUNSET CRATER VOLCANO National Monument 70

TONTO National Monument 71

TUMACACORI National Historical Park 72

TUZIGOOT National Monument 73

WALNUT CANYON National Monument 74

WHITE SANDS National Monument 75

WUPATKI National Monument 76

ZION National Park 77

Acknowledgments 80

Suggested Reading 80

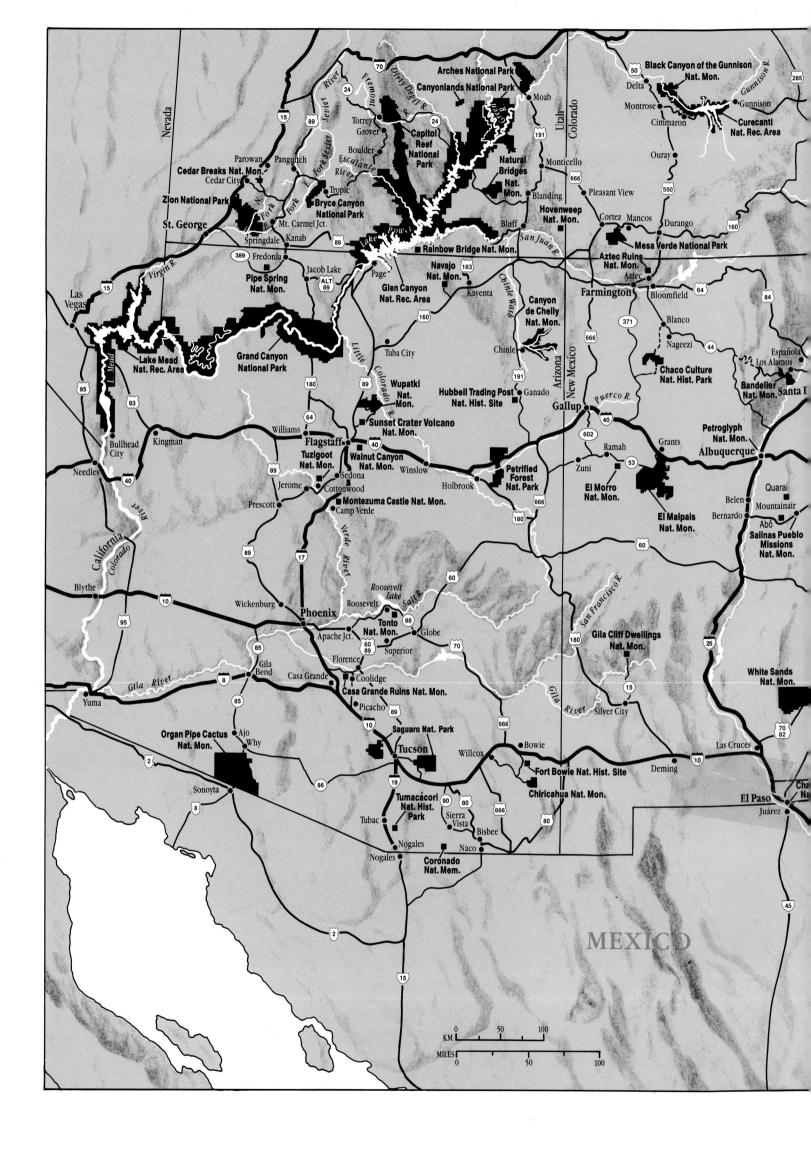

Nevada

Utah

Colorado

70
24
Dirty Devil R.
Fremont R.
Green R.

Arches National Park

Canyonlands National Park • Moab

Black Canyon of the Gunnison
Nat. Mon.
50
Delta
Gunnison R.
285

15
89
Sevier River

Torrey
Grover
24
Capitol Reef National Park

191

Montrose
Cimmaron
Gunnison
Ouray
Curecanti Nat. Rec. Area

Boulder
Escalante

Natural Bridges Nat. Mon.

• Monticello
666
• Pleasant View

Cedar Breaks Nat. Mon.
Parowan • Panguitch
Cedar City
E. Fork Sevier River
Tropic

N. Fork
Fork

Bryce Canyon National Park

Blanding
Hovenweep Nat. Mon.

550
Durango
160
Cortez
Mancos

Zion National Park

St. George

Mt. Carmel Jct.
Springdale
Kanab
89

Lake Powell

Bluff
San Juan R.

Mesa Verde National Park

Aztec Ruins Nat. Mon.
Aztec
64
84

Virgin R.
389
Fredonia
Jacob Lake
ALT 89

Pipe Spring Nat. Mon.
Page
Rainbow Bridge Nat. Mon.

Navajo Nat. Mon.
163

Chinle Wash

Farmington
Bloomfield
371
Blanco

Las Vegas
15

L. Mead

Glen Canyon Nat. Rec. Area

Kayenta

Canyon de Chelly Nat. Mon.
Chinle

666
Nageezi
44

Española
Los Alamos

95
93

Lake Mead Nat. Rec. Area

Grand Canyon National Park

160
Tuba City
Little Colorado R.

191

666

Chaco Culture Nat. Hist. Park

Bandelier Nat. Mon. Santa Fe

Bullhead City
Kingman
180

Wupatki Nat. Mon.

Hubbell Trading Post Nat. Hist. Site • Ganado

Arizona
New Mexico
Gallup
Puerco R.
40

Petroglyph Nat. Mon.

Needles
89

64
Williams

Sunset Crater Volcano Nat. Mon.

602
Ramah
Grants
Albuquerque

Flagstaff
40

California
Colorado River

Tuzigoot Nat. Mon.
Sedona

Walnut Canyon Nat. Mon.
Winslow

Petrified Forest Nat. Park

53
Zuni
El Morro Nat. Mon.

Quarai

89
Jerome
Cottonwood
Holbrook

666
180

Belen
Mountainair

Prescott

Montezuma Castle Nat. Mon.
Camp Verde

El Malpais Nat. Mon.

Abó
Bernardo

Salinas Pueblo Missions Nat. Mon.

89
17
Verde River

Roosevelt Lake
Salt R.
60

60

Blythe
10

Wickenburg

Phoenix
Roosevelt

Tonto Nat. Mon.
88
Globe

Gila Cliff Dwellings Nat. Mon.

25

95

Apache Jct.
60 89
Superior
70

San Francisco R.

White Sands Nat. Mon.

Gila River
8
Gila Bend

Florence
Casa Grande Ruins Nat. Mon.
Coolidge
Casa Grande

Gila River
15
Silver City

85

Picacho
89

Yuma
85

Organ Pipe Cactus Nat. Mon.
Ajo
Why

10
Saguaro Nat. Park
Tucson

Willcox
• Bowie

70
82
Las Cruces

2

86

Fort Bowie Nat. Hist. Site
Deming
10

Sonoyta
19

Chiricahua Nat. Mon.

El Paso

8

Tumacácori Nat. Hist. Park
Tubac
90
80
Sierra Vista
666

80

Juárez

Nogales
Nogales
Naco
Bisbee
80

Coronado Nat. Mem.

MEXICO

45

KM. 0 ——— 50 ——— 100

MILES 0 ——— 50 ——— 100

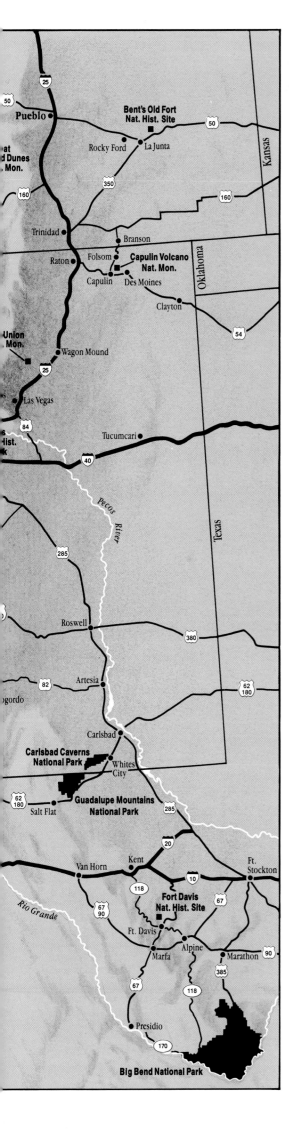

"This is the most beautiful place on earth."

With these simple yet evocative words, author Edward Abbey began *Desert Solitaire*, a moving tribute to Utah's Arches National Park and surrounding country. While Abbey agreed that such opinions are certainly personal, many contend that the Southwest contains a disproportionate number of *special places*, and that a good number of these can be found within the region's national parks.

Not only does the Southwest boast the highest concentration of national parks in the nation, but the variety and diversity of experiences available here may be unparalleled. From awe-inspiring views at Grand Canyon National Park, to spiritual adventures among Anasazi Indian ruins at Mesa Verde National Park, the possibilities for discovery are almost limitless.

Although we often think of the Southwest as *desert country*, this is also a land of bitter cold winters, violent summer thunderstorms, and gale-force winds. It may come as a surprise that winter snows are not uncommon at southern Arizona's Saguaro National Park, or that hot weather can be found even at the 10,000-foot elevation of Utah's Cedar Breaks National Monument. Yet the one defining quality that all of this country shares is dryness — a factor that not only determines the topography and life forms found in the Southwest, but also the remarkable state of preservation at the historic and prehistoric sites now protected by the National Park Service.

When exploring national parks — large or small — we encourage you to take your time; your appreciation will be greatly enhanced. And while these parks are ours to enjoy, they are also ours to preserve. We would do well to treat each one as "the most beautiful place on earth."

■

MAPS This large map of the Southwest was designed to be used for general trip planning; the more detailed access maps will aid you in reaching individual national parks. We suggest you also travel with a good road map. Most parks offer site specific maps and appropriate maps for hiking.

ENTRANCE FEES Many national parks today charge entrance fees. The amount varies depending on the park and in some cases the time of year. An annual Golden Eagle Pass is sold, which allows unlimited access to all national park areas for occupants of a vehicle. A similar free Golden Age Passport is available to anyone over 62, as is a Golden Access Passport for disabled people.

PETS Pets are permitted on leash in most national parks but in limited areas, and not in public buildings, or on trails, or in the backcountry. Horseback riding is allowed in some of the larger parks, by permit only. We advise calling in advance for specific information.

ARCHES NATIONAL PARK

Delicate Arch.

VISITOR INFORMATION

114 sq. mi. Entrance fee. Open year-round; spring, fall, and winter are best times—summers are scorching. Visitor center just off Highway 191 near Moab, open 8 A.M. to 4:30 P.M., with extended hours seasonally. Audiovisual and interpretive programs, exhibits, bookstore. Paved road through park with many turnouts. Mountain biking allowed on established roads only. Hiking trails marked by cairns lead to park features. Backcountry camping by permit. Bring plenty of water and wear a hat— this is the desert. Devils Garden Campground fills up early each day in peak season; campground also available in Canyonlands National Park's Island in the Sky District (no water); limited group sites, by reservation only. Nearby Moab has full services. For more information, write: Superintendent, Arches National Park, P.O. Box 907, Moab, UT 84532; or telephone (435) 259-8161. www.nps.gov/arch

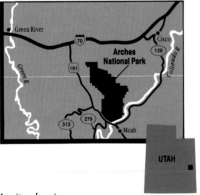

Juniper berries.

The gravity-defying wonders of natural rock arches have always sparked the human imagination. That Mother Nature and immense stretches of time created such geologic marvels is inspiring, even humbling. Although many places in the Southwest boast natural rock spans, Arches National Park holds the world record—more than 1,700 at last count. It was for the beauty and variety of its fiery-hued arches, windows, spires, balanced rocks, fins, and canyons that this region became a national monument in 1929, and a full-fledged national park in 1971.

The carved forms found within these 114 square miles owe their origins to the westward migration over 150 million years of a layer of salt many thousands of feet thick. This salt deposit resulted from the evaporation of seawater in a huge depression called the Paradox Basin. As debris from the adjoining Uncompahgre Uplift shed into the basin and compacted, the underlying salt became "plastic" and flowed away from the pressure. As the salt mass encountered ancient fault blocks, however, it was pushed up through the overlying rock into domes (diapirs). Joints formed along the fault lines. Groundwater entered these cracks and dissolved the salt, thereby causing the domes to collapse and creating the Salt and Cache valleys at the heart of Arches.

Water, ice, and wind continued to enter the joints, widening them and eventually sculpting rock "fins" like those seen in the Fiery Furnace. Erosion eventually exposed the reddish-brown Entrada Sandstone, which seems to lend itself to the crumbling and flaking required to create windows, arches, and spires. Stone towers along Park Avenue, world-famous Delicate Arch, and the record-setting span of Landscape Arch, among others, slowly formed, underlaid by the erosion-resistant, dune-formed Navajo Sandstone.

Despite a 3,960- to 5,653-foot elevation range, and a scant eight inches of annual rainfall, plants and animals abound in this high desert. Moister pockets of soil allow tough trees like juniper and pinyon to grow. Hardy blackbrush appears in areas of gravelly spots, with various grasses gaining a foothold in deeper sandy areas. Sand dunes foster scrub oak and old-man sage, and in the salt valleys, salt-tolerant shrubs like seepweed and pickleweed find a home. Even the soil is alive, with a covering of dark, crusted earth formed by blue-green algae, bacteria, and lichen. These patches create delicate new soil and prevent

erosion of existing soil. Noticeable, too, are choking rafts of Mormon tea and snakeweed, epidemic throughout the Southwest following years of overgrazing. Many plants thrive in the shady, infrequent seeps and streams that water the desert. Tamarisk, cottonwood, and willow, as well as hanging gardens of maidenhair fern, columbine, monkeyflower, and primrose inhabit these riparian troves. In the open, yucca, evening primrose, sand verbena, Indian paintbrush, curly dock, and larkspur punctuate the subtle desert tones.

The kangaroo rat survives desert extremes by efficiently metabolizing water from seeds and burrowing into cool sand. Likewise, the spadefoot toad burrows deep in potholes and awaits infrequent rainstorms to reproduce. Noisy pinyon jays and the pleasant descending pitch of the canyon wren punctuate the desert silence. Rarely sighted are golden eagles and peregrine falcons, while coyotes, kit foxes, antelope ground squirrels, and jackrabbits are ubiquitous.

Arches has hosted many human travelers and some settlers. From A.D. 1000 to 1300, Fremont Indians hunted and gathered here, leaving unique rock art on the walls of Courthouse Wash. Ute Indians were well established in the region by the 1830s and 1840s when travelers on the Old Spanish Trail crossed the Colorado River near present-day Moab. Mormons founded Moab in 1855 but were prevented by Ute incursions from permanently settling until the 1870s. Rail lines linked Utah with the rest of the country in the 1880s; they also played a key role in the creation of Arches National Monument in the twenties, when a local prospector suggested the dramatic Klondike Bluffs be promoted as a scenic stopping point for rail passengers traveling in the West. Crusty Civil War veteran John Wesley Wolfe and his son eked out a lonely existence as ranchers among the arches in 1888. Their cabin, close to Salt Wash, survives as an example of early Western cattle ranching.

Landscape Arch.

Petroglyphs in Salt Wash.

Wolfe Ranch cabin, ca. 1906.

Sandstone fins of Devils Garden.

Visitors to the park today enter by way of Highway 191, past the visitor center and through the distinctive Moab Fault. From here, a paved road and a number of side roads, four-wheel-drive routes, and hiking trails lead to the park's features, with overlooks along the way. More accessible than nearby Canyonlands, Arches has its off-the-beaten-track areas too. Isolated in the northwest portion of the park, Klondike Bluffs, the park's original tourist attraction, is now ironically one of its least visited areas.

AZTEC RUINS NATIONAL MONUMENT

Reconstructed great kiva.

VISITOR INFORMATION

27 acres. Entrance fee. Open 8 A.M. to 5 P.M.,
6 P.M. Memorial Day–Labor Day. Visitor center:
audiovisual program, exhibits, telecommunications
device for the deaf (TDD), interpretive activities,
bookstore. No camping. Picnicking allowed.
Food and lodging available in Aztec or nearby
Bloomfield. For more information, write:
Superintendent, Aztec Ruins National Monument,
P.O. Box 640, Aztec, NM 87410; or telephone
(505) 334-6174. www.nps.gov/azru

Situated in the fertile Animas River valley in the San Juan Basin of northern New Mexico, Aztec Ruins National Monument makes a fascinating stop for visitors to nearby, larger parks at Chaco Canyon and Mesa Verde. Exciting new studies of Aztec's architectural and cultural remains are now revealing that a unique blending of Chacoan and Mesa Verdean Anasazi cultures took place here between the twelfth and fourteenth centuries.

Archeologists believe that Aztec Ruins (misnamed by pioneer settlers who thought the site was Aztec in origin) was built in the early 1100s as an outlier, or satellite community, of Chaco Canyon. Such outliers have been found throughout the San Juan Basin, and many were great houses, or community gathering places, probably used by the Chacoans as ceremonial and trade centers. Their location on a large prehistoric road network suggests that they were important supply centers for Chaco Canyon.

Visitors to Aztec can examine a stabilized great house ruin, a reconstructed great kiva, and an unusual tri-walled structure surrounding a kiva, whose meaning is still unclear. Tree-ring dating has revealed that the great kiva was contemporaneous with the great kivas at Pueblo Bonito in Chaco Canyon and therefore probably used for similar purposes. Aztec's great kiva is now the largest reconstructed structure of its kind in the Southwest. A second unexcavated pueblo with a great kiva, and an additional two, perhaps three, tri-walled structures are also evident at the monument; these are not currently open to the public. Several more great houses, kivas, and associated residences have been uncovered near

Aztec, indicating that it was a larger and more complex community than once thought.

Archeologist Earl Morris, who excavated Aztec between 1916 and 1923, concluded that the Chacoans abandoned Aztec in the late 1100s, and the site apparently stood empty for about twenty-five years until it was reoccupied by the Mesa Verdeans. Now, with information from more sophisticated dating methods, archeologists believe that the Aztec region was never completely abandoned. Instead, a transitional culture existed here that eventually exhibited Mesa Verde cultural traits. During this Mesa Verdean period a new style of pottery was manufactured, more rooms were added, and some rooms in the pueblo were remodeled. Mesa Verde architecture at Aztec is distinguished by a looser, less complex building style than that used by earlier Chacoan masons, who built strong walls consisting of bands of small, tightly wedged rocks sandwiched between larger stones.

Aztec's Anasazi inhabitants were attracted to this valley because of its favorable location and fertile, irrigable soil. They cultivated typically Southwestern crops and supplemented their diet with game and wild plants. As contact with other cultures grew, the people of Aztec traded their pottery and other goods for precious turquoise, salt, cotton cloth, abalone shell, and other goods.

Identification of ceramics has provided vital clues to the sequence of cultural development in the Southwest, and this has been particularly true at Aztec. Pottery found here ranges from the hatched designs and chalky surfaces of Chacoan ceramics, to an intermediate style known as McElmo black-on-white, to the distinctive, solid black-on-white designs and "ticked" rims characteristic of Mesa Verdean ceramics.

Population pressure, shrinking natural resources, and severe drought in the 1200s may all have influenced final abandonment of the Aztec pueblo by its Anasazi occupants. They apparently moved south and joined pueblos on the more reliable Rio Grande drainage.

Chacoan-style olla.

When anthropologist Adolph Bandelier first was led into Frijoles Canyon in 1880 he enthused that it was "the grandest thing I ever saw." Many would agree with Bandelier's estimation of the area that he explored and which came to bear his name. From canyon bottom to mountain top, welcoming Bandelier National Monument offers abundant archeological riches and breathtaking scenic beauty, within easy striking distance of Santa Fe, in north-central New Mexico.

Hundreds of ruins of masonry structures and cave shelters dot Frijoles and other canyons and mesas throughout Bandelier. Several thousand years ago, the region was used by Paleo-Indian hunters and eventually by Archaic hunter-gatherers, who wandered through its sheltered canyons in search of game and wild plants. Then, around the time of Christ, small family groups of Basketmaker Anasazi began to settle in the canyons, living in semisubterranean pit houses. They cultivated corn, squash, beans, and melons and continued to hunt and forage like their predecessors. As yet, little evidence has been found of these cultures in the monument itself, although it is likely that they used its sheltered canyons. Succeeding generations of these fledgling farmers were to remain for many centuries.

Long House Ruin in Frijoles Canyon.

Mule deer.

Early in the twelfth century, the settlers may have been joined by members of the Anasazi culture fleeing the arid Four Corners region. Advanced Anasazi masonry construction, successful farming techniques, and an increase in population marked a cultural explosion among the people of the Jemez Mountains. Using rough tools made from local basalt, they scooped out dwellings from the soft tuff walls of the Pajarito Plateau, and, innovatively, they fronted the cavelike rooms with multistory masonry buildings supported by wooden beams. These villages, visible today for more than a mile along the talus slopes of Frijoles Canyon, employed warming southern exposures, small rooms, and protected openings, making them relatively snug homes. On your walk around the canyon, be sure to check out Ceremonial Cave one mile from the visitor center. Located 140 feet

above canyon bottom, it once sheltered a cliff dwelling and kiva. You can climb up to view this spectacular site, but the ladders leading to it are not for the faint-hearted.

In the thirteenth century, the Anasazi started to construct Tyuonyi, a circular, two-story pueblo in the bottom of Frijoles Canyon. This high-walled town, which apparently boomed in the fifteenth century, sheltered a population of about 100 people. The women performed masonry work, made pottery, and prepared food, while the men farmed and hunted, wove cloth, and attended to important seasonal ceremonies in the kivas. By the early 1500s, though, the residents withdrew from the area, never to return. They almost certainly became the dwellers of the Cochiti and San

(continued)

VISITOR INFORMATION

50 sq. mi. Entrance fee. Open 9 A.M. to 5:30 P.M. (winter), longer hours in summer. Visitor center in Frijoles Canyon: audiovisual programs, exhibits, interpretive activities, bookstore. Snack bar. Gift shop. 95 campsites (March through November) and group campground (mid-April through October). Food and lodging at nearby Los Alamos. For more information, write: Superintendent, Bandelier National Monument, HCR 1, Box 1, Suite 15, Los Alamos, NM 87544; or telephone (505) 672-3861. www.nps.gov/band

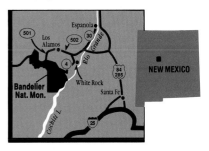

Cavate dwelling on Ruins Trail.

Kiva in Ceremonial Cave.

Scarlet gilia.

Lower Falls, Frijoles Canyon.

Ildefonso pueblos on the Rio Grande. In the words of this song, a Pueblo Indian remembers his ancestors:

> Now sleep the old ones
> From far away they traveled to Frijoles
> Far away now their children are . . .

Religious sites in the monument, such as the Stone Lions shrine, are still used by the Pueblo people today.

Frijoles Canyon (named for the beans grown here by early residents) was carved by Frijoles Creek, which descends southeast from the Jemez Mountains to meet the Rio Grande. The surrounding 10,000-foot Jemez peaks are actually the rim of an ancient volcano. Valle Grande, a part of the enormous caldera, stretches along the road to Jemez Springs. Just over a million years ago, eruptions from this volcano covered much of the surrounding area with ash that hardened into a rock called tuff. The Pajarito Plateau, through which Frijoles Canyon was carved, is composed entirely of this volcanic material. Although the monument was set aside to protect prehistoric Indian structures, Bandelier's rich geologic history is a constant subtext throughout the monument. Of particular interest are the formations visible from the Falls Trail, south of the visitor center. The trailguide describing the geology of the area is an excellent companion for this hike.

Nearly three-quarters of Bandelier National Monument is wilderness spanning 5,000- to 10,000-foot elevations, and trips into the backcountry along maintained hiking trails are highly recommended. Canyons and changing vistas await backpackers, along with the opportunity to visit a variety of plant communities. Cottonwoods and box elders thrive in the canyon bottom; yucca, saltbush, and walking stick cholla hug the dry canyon walls; and pinyon and juniper grow thick on the mesa tops, giving way to lofty ponderosa pine and fir in the high country. The protected Jemez Mountain salamander in upper Frijoles Canyon is one of the many animal species—large and small—that call Bandelier home; you may even glimpse black bear, elk, or even, rarely, a mountain lion at higher elevations. Bandelier's visitor center, with many fine interpretive materials, offers an excellent orientation to this rich and varied site.

BENT'S OLD FORT
NATIONAL HISTORIC SITE

Bent's Old Fort, reconstructed to its appearance in 1846.

Blacksmith shop.

Between the years of 1833 and 1849, Bent's Old Fort, a trading post on the Colorado plains, was the Southwest's most influential international meeting place, bringing together Americans, Mexicans, and Native Americans in a mutually beneficial trading environment. During these early days on the frontier, peace of a sort, prosperity, and growing cultural interaction forged the Southwest's reputation as an attractive destination for many an American dreamer.

In 1831, Frenchman Ceran Saint Vrain and brothers William and Charles Bent pooled their resources and fur trading expertise and formed Bent, St. Vrain and Company. The firm built its headquarters in Colorado's Arkansas River Valley, next to where the mountain branch of the Santa Fe Trail headed south into Mexico and surrounded by Plains Indian territory, allowing them to capitalize on international trade. The trading center was built like a castle, with thick adobe walls and armed turrets. Inside were a plaza, warehouses, corral, kitchen, dining room, billiard room, owners' living quarters, and accommodations for traders, guests, trappers, and laborers. Blacksmith and carpentry shops were used for wagon repairs and shoeing of livestock. The trading post's main business took place in trading and meeting rooms.

Charles Bent bought trade goods in Saint Louis and spent much time on the trail between that city and company stores in Santa Fe and Taos. Saint Vrain oversaw the Santa Fe operation and bought gold and silver coin, Navajo blankets, and exotic foods from vendors for the Plains Indian and Mexican markets. Bent's Fort was managed by William Bent, known for his skillful dealings with Indian and Mexican traders, mountain men, and travelers staying at the fort. He offered the trading

post as a safe meeting place for settling intertribal disputes. Fury among local Southern Cheyenne, Arapahoe, Ute, Apache, Kiowa, and Comanche tribes at Anglo encroachment on traditional hunting grounds was somewhat mitigated by trade that brought guns, Mexican horses, Navajo blankets, tools, and coveted domestic items in return for buffalo robes.

This period of peaceful trading ended in late 1845 when Texas became a state. Bent's Fort was commandeered by General Stephen Kearny's Army of the West, under orders to secure New Mexico for the Union during the 1846 War with Mexico. Kearny's easy victory over Santa Fe, and the resulting territorial expansion, moved the United States one step closer to continental unification, yet its consequences brought many changes for the plains dwellers. Charles Bent was appointed the first United States governor of New Mexico, but he was killed several months later in the 1847 Taos Rebellion. Saint Vrain sold his share in the company and moved permanently to Santa Fe. William Bent remained at the fort, but important Indian trade diminished. Then, a severe outbreak of cholera almost obliterated the native population. Following a devastating fire in 1849, he and his family left the trading post forever.

Bent's Old Fort became a national historic site in 1960. Fifteen years later, the National Park Service meticulously reconstructed the fort and its thirty-three rooms with the help of 1846 visitor diaries and sketches and archeological investigations. Today, costumed interpreters and a program of special living history events bring to life the sights and sounds of an era in American history when anything seemed possible.

VISITOR INFORMATION

1.2 sq. mi. Entrance fee. Open 8 A.M. to 5:30 P.M. (summer); 9 A.M. to 4 P.M. (winter). Visitor center is in the Indian Trade Room where visitors view a 20-minute film on fort; information, bookstore, and gift shop also available. 45-minute guided tours through reconstructed fur trading post hourly, as well as historic demonstrations daily in summer. Special living history events throughout the year are of particular interest. No camping, but picnicking allowed. Nearest visitor services in La Junta or Las Animas. For more information, write: Superintendent, Bent's Old Fort National Historic Site, 35110 Highway 194 East, La Junta, CO 81050-9523; or telephone (719) 383-5010. www.nps.gov/beol

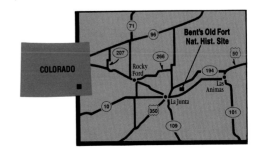

BIG BEND
NATIONAL PARK

The Sierra Quemada seen from the south rim of the Chisos Mountains.

VISITOR INFORMATION

1,200 sq. mi. Entrance fee. Open year-round. Park headquarters at Panther Junction. Visitor centers at Panther Junction and Rio Grande Village open roughly 8 A.M. to 5 P.M.: exhibits, interpretive activities, information, bookstore; ranger stations at Castolon, The Basin, and Persimmon Gap. Exhibits also at Barton Warnock Environmental Education Center at Lajitas and Desert Garden outside park. For information on Big Bend publications and seminars, contact Big Bend Natural History Association at (915) 477-2236. 3 paved roads lead into park, but distances from nearest major U.S. towns are great. Scenic drives, picnicking, hiking, birding, river trips, and fishing. Hiking trails for all abilities. Backcountry hiking and camping by permit only. Take adequate water, sun protection, food, and a topographical map. Beware of desert extremes and occasional rattlesnakes. River rafting and guides available through concessionaires outside park. Main campgrounds at Rio Grande Village and Chisos Basin; and campground also at Cottonwood. 189 campsites on first-come, first-served basis. Groups may reserve 90 days ahead. Concessionaire-run Chisos Mountain Lodge with gift shop in The Basin; call (915) 477-2291 for reservations. Gas and minor auto repairs at Panther Junction. Nearest visitor services at Study Butte, Lajitas, and Terlingua. For more information, write: Superintendent, Big Bend National Park, TX 79834; or telephone (915) 477-2251. www.nps.gov/bibe

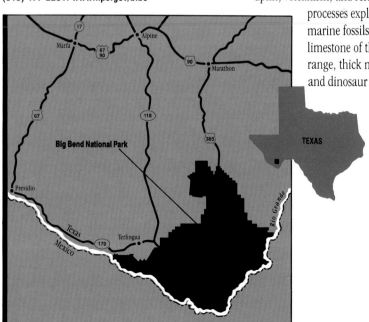

Texas's Big Bend National Park not only preserves a magnificently diverse section of the vast Chihuahuan Desert but has also been designated a World Biosphere Reserve in recognition of its unique place in the planet's ecology. In addition to its natural riches, Big Bend is one of the country's most startlingly beautiful parks. Here, arid desert lowlands are pierced by temperate mountains and the winding Rio Grande, which makes its way through three limestone canyons along the Mexican border.

Big Bend's unusual topography is the result of roughly 300 million years of climatic and geologic changes. Warm seas covered the area for millennia, followed by periods of sedimentation, uplift, volcanism, and relentless erosion. These processes explain why there are marine fossils embedded in the uplifted limestone of the Sierra del Carmen range, thick mud shales at Hot Springs, and dinosaur remains in the badlands near the park's Maverick entrance. For eons, the 38-million-year-old igneous cores of the 8,000-foot Chisos Mountains were hidden under thick sedimentary layers. Now, however, erosion has exposed their fiery origins. Nearby lava eruptions formed the weathered, blocky peaks of the South Rim of the Chisos, and hot ash from volcanic craters fused into tuffaceous formations like the Mule Ears. Mammals replaced dinosaurs during this Cenozoic Period, and lush grasslands covered much of the Big Bend area. The wetter climate caused rivers loaded with abrasive sediments to bear down on the mountains, as they scoured paths to the sea. The ancestor of the modern-day Rio Conchos, which rises in Mexico and joins the sluggish Rio Grande, was probably responsible for the splendid, 1,500-foot-deep Santa Elena, Mariscal, and Boquillas canyons. These sheer river cuts first began to be explored in the mid-1800s, when succeeding groups of American surveyors floated first Mariscal, then Santa Elena, and finally Boquillas in 1889.

Although hot and dry, the 1,800- to 4,500-foot elevations of the Chihuahuan Desert are home to many plants and animals. Coyotes, kit foxes, snakes, peccaries, and jackrabbits beat the heat by hunting at night, but day hikers may sometimes see a western coachwhip snake or an earless lizard sidling along. Water comes and goes quickly, so desert inhabitants employ many survival methods. Kangaroo rats metabolize their own water supply from dry seeds, and spadefoot toads burrow underground, waiting to lay their eggs in rainwater pools. Cacti store water in expandable waxy trunks protected by spines. In spring, their flowers attract winged pollinators, such as bats and birds, and by summer many, like the prickly pear, have edible fruits. Candelilla, or wax plants, which prevent moisture loss by coating their exteriors with a waxy sap, have long been used to make commercial wax and even supported a factory at Glenn Springs in the early 1900s. Ocotillo and agave punctuate large areas dominated by hardy creosote bush. Especially noticeable is the giant dagger yucca, whose splendid blooms invigorate Dagger Flats every few years. A memorable sight, too, are carpets of Texas bluebonnets (known as lupine elsewhere), narrow-leaf globemallow, and prickly poppy, which begin to bloom in late winter and may brighten the park into late spring.

At least 434 bird species have been recorded at Big Bend, more than in any other national park. Birders are best rewarded in the park's streamside, or riparian, environments. Colorful summer tanagers, Bell's vireos, painted buntings, and vermilion flycatchers, to name but a few, reside among the green cottonwoods, willows, and tamarisk lining the river. Bank beavers share this home with several kinds of turtles and Big Bend gambusia, an endangered fish.

The last Ice Age and the warmer, drier climate that followed forced wildlife and plants to retreat to the mountains. Relict forests of western yellow pine, bigtooth maple, and Arizona cypress associated with the cooler north now exist here in isolation. The mountains support mountain sage, Chisos agave, and oak found nowhere else in the world; they also shelter Carmen Mountains whitetail deer, endangered peregrine falcons, and very rarely a golden eagle. The proximity of Mexico means that Mexican trees, such as the drooping juniper, grow alongside American cousins, and rare birds, such as the colima warbler, find a warm weather home in Boot Canyon. Other migratory species, such as Big Bend's mountain lions and growing numbers of Mexican black bear, range freely across park and international borders in search of prey, presenting special challenges for park officials. An agreement between Mexico and the United States signed in 1989 has established a bilateral committee to address problems of protecting resources along the international border. The Rio Grande defines the park's southern boundary with Mexico for 107 miles, then flows northeastward through a wildlife management area. Since 1978, the park service has administered 127 miles of river east of the park as the Rio Grande Wild and Scenic River, an area popular with rafters.

Hunter-gatherer Indians of the Desert Archaic culture lived in the desert country of Big Bend for 6,000 years, their descendants finally becoming sedentary farmers and settling into villages here around the 1200s. The Chisos Indians who inhabited the area in early historic times apparently reverted to supplementing seasonal crops with hunting and gathering, before being displaced by raiding Mescalero Apaches in the eighteenth century. In the 1500s and 1600s, Spanish exploration did not yield the expected treasure north of the Rio Grande, but presidios were built in northern Mexico in the late 1700s in an unsuccessful attempt to combat Apache raids. After gaining vast new territory from Mexico in 1848, the United States built nearby Fort Davis and other Southwestern forts to protect settlers and travelers from Apache and Comanche raiding parties crossing Texas, the western Big Bend area, and into Mexico. Peace treaties were eventually signed with the Indian nations in 1886, and settlers slowly migrated toward the fertile Rio Grande floodplain. By 1901, a Mexican farmer named Cipriano Hernandez was selling extra produce from his small adobe home in Castolon to neighboring cotton farmers and miners. The trading post is still visible at Castolon today. Such communities were frequently raided by Mexican bandits following the outbreak of the Mexican Revolution in 1911. In 1916, a particularly severe attack at Glenn Springs caused the U.S. Cavalry to build a fort there, which was abandoned when fighting ceased.

Dagger yuccas in bloom, Dagger Flats.

The Rio Grande and Chisos Mountains.

Roadrunner.

Cattle ranching became big business in the Big Bend during the twenties and thirties, but at a cost to the desert grasslands and wildlife dependent on them. Overgrazing and trampling destroyed fragile desert habitat and allowed weedy shrubs to take hold. Big Bend became a national park in 1944, and gradually portions of grassland have returned, but protection of habitat for the approximately 5,000 kinds of plants and animals here remains a priority.

BLACK CANYON OF THE GUNNISON NATIONAL MONUMENT

VISITOR INFORMATION

32 sq. mi. South Rim open year-round (open to Gunnison Point in winter). North Rim (gravel road) closed by snow in winter. Gunnison Point Visitor Center on South Rim open daily, 8 A.M. to 6 P.M. (summer); 9 A.M. to 3 P.M. (winter); information, exhibits, interpretive programs in summer. Rim drives, nature trail, birding, fishing, steep hikes into inner canyon, cross-country skiing, advanced technical rock climbing, some kayaking. Permits required for backcountry hikes, climbing, and kayaking. 102 campsites, South Rim; 13 campsites, North Rim (both closed in winter). Rim House on the South Rim sells food and souvenirs in summer. Lodging and restaurants in nearby towns of Montrose, Delta, Paonia, and Hotchkiss. For more information, write: Superintendent, Black Canyon of the Gunnison National Monument, 102 Elk Creek, Gunnison, CO 81230; or telephone (970) 641-2337. www.nps.gov/blca

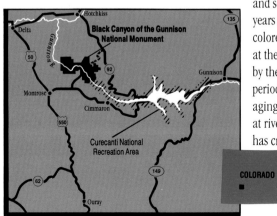

The Gunnison River in the Black Canyon.

Black Canyon of the Gunnison National Monument preserves twelve of the deepest and most scenic miles of the dark-walled, imposing Black Canyon, which runs fifty-three miles through west-central Colorado. But if it hadn't been for the good people of Montrose, Colorado, and surrounding communities, the dramatic beauty of the Black Canyon may never have received federal protection. Their four-year campaign paid off in 1933 when President Herbert Hoover proclaimed the canyon a national monument.

The soft volcanic and harder metamorphic rocks of Black Canyon have been slowly cut through by the Gunnison River, which flows across the Uncompahgre Plateau to meet the Colorado River. The canyon walls are primarily composed of dark Precambrian-era rocks—crystalline gneiss and schist—which were formed some 1.7 billion years ago. These rocks are marbled with light-colored igneous (magma) intrusions, as evidenced at the Painted Wall. Two million years of scouring by the Gunnison River, especially effective during periods of flooding, left this narrow crevasse averaging 2,000 feet deep and as little as forty feet wide at river level at the Narrows. The geological gash has created an impasse for travel in the region.

Prehistoric Indians and wandering Utes used the canyon rims, but Spanish explorers avoided Black Canyon. United States Army Captain John W. Gunnison, for whom the river was named, bypassed the gorge during a survey of the region for an easier southerly route. Not until the famous Hayden Expedition of 1873–1874 was the chasm first recorded by white men. In 1882, the Denver and Rio Grande Railroad commissioned Byron H. Bryant to survey the Black Canyon west of the Cimarron River. After two months of arduous labor, Bryant concluded that construction of a railway in this part of the canyon was impractical.

By 1901, settlers in the Uncompahgre Valley clamored for reliable water sources for ranching and agriculture. After an unsuccessful attempt to resurvey the canyon in 1900, Abraham Lincoln Fellows and William Torrence completed an inner canyon trip in 1901 to determine the possibility of diverting water from the Gunnison River. Their river run confirmed that an irrigation tunnel was indeed feasible. In 1909, President Taft dedicated the 5.5-mile-long Gunnison Diversion Tunnel—a remarkable feat of engineering for the times. Today, the three dams within Curecanti National Recreation Area (upstream of the monument) have slowed erosion of the canyon, even as they have provided needed water storage and recreation opportunities.

The thirty-two square miles of the monument are largely wilderness, ideal for hiking, camping, and observing wildlife. The Gunnison River, proclaimed a Gold Medal Water by the state of Colorado, provides excellent trout fishing for those willing to make the arduous trek to canyon bottom. During your stay, you are likely to see mule deer, chipmunks, ground squirrels, and marmots on the canyon rim. Coyotes are generally heard, not seen, as they hunt rabbits and other rodents at nightfall. Count yourself lucky to glimpse cougar, bobcat, or bighorn sheep—they avoid human contact whenever possible. Bird-watching is amply rewarded, though. A plethora of vocal pinyon jays and black-billed magpies inhabit Gambel oak and serviceberry trees, while the vertical cliffs are home to white-throated swifts, swallows, golden eagles, red-tailed hawks, and even the rare peregrine falcon. Several kinds of snakes and lizards reside at canyon bottom, where insects are plentiful.

South Rim Drive affords many stunning overlooks of the twists and turns of the canyon. The North Rim, though closed in winter, provides a pleasant alternative to the South Rim, with less traffic and spectacular viewpoints from near-vertical cliffs.

View from the
Queen's Garden
Trail.

Manzanita.

L ong ago, according to Paiute Indian myth, the animal Legend People who lived in Bryce Canyon displeased Coyote. In anger, he turned them all to rock, and such they remain to this day, huddled silently along the sheer cliffs of this limestone plateau in southern Utah.

Bryce's surreal geomorphic forms can be explained by geology and time, but as changes in light and perspective make this magical landscape come alive, it is easy to find yourself seduced into believing fiction rather than fact. In fact, Bryce is not a canyon at all, but a series of fourteen amphitheaters carved out of the eastern face of the Paunsaugunt Plateau. Here, the roseate rocks of the Claron Formation predominate. These soft sedimentary layers were originally silts, sands, and the limy skeletons of freshwater lake creatures deposited in 2,000-foot-thick beds nearly 60 million years ago. Minerals gradually cemented the particles into the strata exposed here and in nearby Cedar Breaks National Monument.

These dramatic canyonlands began forming around 13 million years ago. At that time, the land slowly rose up, then split along several fault lines. As the elements went to work on the exposed plateaus, the rock candy formations of Bryce began to take shape. Water, snow, and ice carved deeply into the soft rock, etching spires, pinnacles, windows, arches, and natural bridges. Adding to the drama, iron and manganese in the rock oxidized, bathing the already phantasmagorical hoodoos in a rainbow wash of color. There is order in this seemingly random profusion of tablelands. Bryce is considered the top "step" of a geological Grand Staircase: a series of mesas rising one above another from the Grand Canyon to Bryce Canyon, each step composed of rock strata of a different color. Bryce is part of what are popularly known as the Pink Cliffs in this staircase.

The 6,600- to 9,100-foot elevation range fosters three separate life zones at Bryce. In the Upper Sonoran zone (6,600–7,000 feet), pygmy pinyon and juniper trees grow alongside sagebrush. But most of the park experienced by visitors is made up of the 7,000- to 8,500-foot transition zone, with a forest dominated by ponderosa pine. As you reach the Canadian zone at 8,500 feet, the ponderosas give way to white fir and blue spruce and occasional stands of gnarled bristlecone pine. The ancient bristlecones, with lifespans commonly exceeding a thousand years, are rare finds indeed.

Mule deer often venture alongside the road in the early evening, and ground squirrels make constant companions on the various hiking trails. Looking up, you may glimpse red-tailed hawks slowly riding the air currents overhead, in sharp contrast with the darting swoops of swallows en route to their cliff nests. Early summer welcomes a colorful profusion of wildflowers. By June, Indian paintbrush, penstemon, wild iris, and skyrocket gilia rival the canyon for color and beauty.

VISITOR INFORMATION

56 sq. mi. Entrance fee. Park open year-round; lodging and services open mid-May to mid-October only. Visitor center open year-round, except Christmas Day (hours vary seasonally): information, interpretive programs, bookstore. 18-mile rim drive offers 13 overlooks. Park has 9 highly recommended main hikes and several backcountry trails (bring plenty of water). Concessionaire-operated horseback tours. Cross-country skiing and snowshoeing in winter encouraged, but no snow-mobiling allowed. Reserve well in advance for Bryce Canyon Lodge, call (303) 297-2757. 206 campsites in 2 National Park Service campgrounds operated on first-come, first-served basis (some sites available year-round). For more information, write: Superintendent, Bryce Canyon National National Park, Bryce Canyon, UT 84717; or telephone (435) 834-5322. www.nps.gov/brca

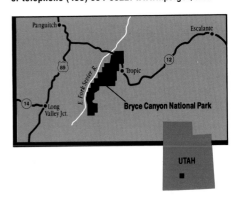

(continued)

The Silent City from Sunset Point.

Indian paintbrush and harebell.

Douglas fir in Wall Street, Navajo Loop Trail.

White-tailed prairie dog.

Prehistoric Anasazi basketmakers and pueblo-builders once lived here, followed by nomadic Paiute hunter-gatherers, who passed through seasonally. The first whites to enter the area were Mormon settlers and American boosters. In the 1870s, Mormon settlers in the Paria Valley to the east were too busy taming the land and building communities to pay much attention to the splendor of the Paunsaugunt Plateau. Nevertheless, Ebenezer Bryce homesteaded close to the cliffs in the mid-1870s, farming and building a logging road that went through the amphitheaters. Locals were quick to call the area Bryce's Canyon.

But it was not until John Wesley Powell's U.S. Geological Survey expeditions of 1872 and 1875–1877 that Bryce's spectacular formations were reported. United States Deputy Surveyor T. C. Bailey thought the amphitheaters made up "one of the wonders of the world." Gradually, word spread, helped along by the U.S. Forest Service in the early 1900s. Roads were built, articles written about the splendors of Bryce, and concessions, such as Tourist's Rest and Bryce Canyon Lodge, opened to serve visitors. Bryce became a national monument in 1923 and achieved national park status in 1928.

This is a small, accessible park, with many of the sights along seventeen miles of sheer cliff face. Thirty-five miles of paved roads and overlooks, and spectacular hiking trails winding through the hoodoos, invite both short- and long-term visits. The magic of Bryce is particularly pronounced on moonlit night hikes into the amphitheaters, but time spent just contemplating at Sunset or Sunrise points is equally rewarding. Winter activities, such as cross-country skiing and snowshoeing, are gaining in popularity here; snowmobiling is allowed in adjoining U.S. Forest Service areas. Transformed under a fresh mantle of snow, the park offers a completely different experience off-season.

CANYON de CHELLY NATIONAL MONUMENT

Canyon de Chelly National Monument lies within the windswept desert of the Navajo Indian reservation in northeastern Arizona. Visitors cross many miles of open plains to reach the monument, where, unexpectedly, the desert floor opens to reveal two deep sandstone canyons of a beauty rivaling that of the Grand Canyon. But even more significant are the many ruins found throughout the canyons, which reflect the importance of this area to successive Indian occupants over the last 2,000 years.

Taking its name from the Navajo word *tsegi*, generally translated as "rock canyon," Canyon de Chelly is owned entirely by the Navajo Nation, making it an unusual member of the national park system. Upkeep and interpretation are joint responsibilities of the Navajo Nation and the National Park Service. Canyon de Chelly continues to hold particular significance for Navajo people, many of whom live here, make pilgrimages, or graze livestock in the canyon bottoms. Visitors have the chance to observe a continuing way of life as well as to discover the area's rich past.

These canyons reveal their secrets slowly; so, a visit of several days is strongly advised. A stop at the visitor center in adjoining Chinle will help you plan your trip. Private Navajo-led back-country tours are an excellent way to learn about the area, as are concessionaire-run half-day and whole-day tours. If you're pressed for time, two thirty-five-mile rim drives will give a superficial overview of the canyons and their ruins. The only public access into the canyon is via a 2.5-mile trail leading to White House Ruins; this restriction is strictly enforced.

Canyon de Chelly and neighboring Canyon del Muerto, up to 1,000 feet deep in places, were carved into the Defiance Plateau by the Rio de Chelly, which flows from the nearby Chuska Mountains into Chinle Wash. The canyon walls consist of the Supai, de Chelly, and Shinarump formations, with the de Chelly Sandstone making up the bulk of what you see. Swirling strata dramatically mirror its ancient sand dune origins. Dark streaks of "desert varnish" are particularly pronounced here, caused primarily by iron and manganese oxides. Juniper-pinyon stands and scrub oak, along with cholla and prickly pear cactus, mark the canyon rims. Also prevalent are rabbitbrush and snakeweed, symptoms of past overgrazing. The high water table at canyon bottom supports cottonwood, willow, and the nonnative Russian olive and tamarisk. Peach trees, first planted by the Hopi, are thriving in the canyon once again after earlier orchards were cut down by the U.S. Army in the 1860s.

(continued)

White House Ruin.

Autumn reflections in Canyon del Muerto.

VISITOR INFORMATION

130 sq. mi. Visitor center open 8 A.M. to 6 P.M. in summer, closing at 5 P.M. in winter: audiovisual program, exhibits, information, bookstore, Ranger-led activities in summer. Free campground, first-come, first-served; group campsites available by reservation. Food and gifts at Thunderbird Lodge. Nearby Chinle offers lodging and several eating establishments. Access into canyon is restricted. Visitors may hike White House Ruin trail unaccompanied, or enter canyon with paid, authorized Navajo guide and visitor's own four-wheel-drive vehicle (arrange through visitor center). Guided half-day/whole-day tours into canyon, available through Thunderbird Lodge, are popular. Horseback riding is also available. Note that Canyon de Chelly is on daylight saving time, in contrast with rest of Arizona. For more information, write: Superintendent, Canyon de Chelly National Monument, Box 588, Chinle, AZ 86503; or telephone (520) 674-5500. www.nps.gov/cach

Spider Rock.

Soaring red-tailed hawk.

Navajo pictograph of Spanish horseman.

Antelope House in Canyon del Muerto.

Anasazi farmers growing corn, squash, and later beans, inhabited the canyons for a thousand years. Among the 700 known prehistoric ruins are pit houses from the earliest centuries A.D. and south-facing, multistoried cliff pueblos, built between the eleventh and late thirteenth centuries. White House and Mummy Cave ruins, with their fascinating rock art, offer few clues to why the Anasazi started to build against and into the cliffs. Perhaps flooding, the need for defense, or lack of land were the reasons. Whatever the environmental or social factors, by the 1200s life in the canyons was apparently becoming intolerable for residents, and a particularly long drought seems to have tipped the balance. The Anasazi abandoned the canyons for good.

Shortly afterward, Hopi farmers began to use the canyons seasonally, followed in the 1700s by Navajo fugitives evading Spanish reprisals for persistent attacks on Rio Grande villages. Massacre Cave in Canyon del Muerto is the site of the 1805 Spanish attack that left 115 Navajo dead. The long shadow of the 1864 Long Walk also reaches here. Kit Carson, under the command of U.S. Army General James Carleton, marched the Navajo to eastern New Mexico in the first "reservation" experiment. After the government failed to suppress Navajo unity, the *Diné* (the People) were allowed to return here for good in 1868.

Nowadays, most young Navajos leave the reservation temporarily for cash jobs, but many older Navajos still farm and graze sheep and goats in the canyons. A Navajo homestead with circular hogan (house), grazing flock, and fruit trees is visible on the White House Ruins Trail. The Navajo are world-renowned for their splendid wool rugs and turquoise jewelry, which are sold at nearby trading posts.

View of Canyonlands and the Colorado River.

With towering desert sculpture and shifting hues, Canyonlands National Park is a land of many contrasts, incapable of compromise, and brings us face to face with our strongest emotions about landscape.

This large park is divided into three units with Y-shaped geographic boundaries defined by the confluence of the mighty Green and Colorado rivers—principal architects of this majestically eroded land. To the north, located between the two rivers, is the 6,000-foot-high Island in the Sky, easily accessible from nearby Moab and providing the best park vistas. Deceptively close in appearance, to the south, is the Needles District, a dreamscape of arches, buttes, spires, and canyons, sprinkled with Indian ruins. More remote still is the wilderness of the Maze District, which lies southwest of where the two rivers converge. Its pristine, deeply gooosenecked canyons, Land of Standing Rocks, and splendid Indian rock art are accessible only by foot, river, or four-wheel-drive dirt roads. The rivers comprise a fourth unit, offering relaxed float trips through meandering canyons above the confluence, and below it, fourteen miles of challenging white-water rafting through Cataract Canyon to Lake Powell. Just east loom the La Sal Mountains. Like the Abajos to the south, and Navajo Mountain and the Henrys to the southwest, erosion has now revealed the igneous beginnings of these 12,000-foot laccolithic (magma-intruded) peaks.

(continued)

VISITOR INFORMATION

527 sq. mi. Open year-round; entrance fees are collected March through Oct. at the Island in the Sky and the Needles. Spring and fall are best times; summers can be hot and stormy. An orientation at visitor centers in the Island in the Sky, the Needles, Moab Information Center, or the Monticello Visitor Center is strongly recommended. Visitor center hours are 8 A.M. to 4:30 P.M. daily (with extended hours seasonally); audiovisual program, information, interpretive activities, and bookstore. Water and visitor facilities unavailable in most of park; come supplied, distances are much greater than they appear. Scenic drives; mountain biking on established roads; hiking on rugged trails of different lengths marked by rock cairns, many leading to park features. Do not hike alone; bring water and wear a hat. Island in the Sky is most accessible, with paved road and turnouts, but Willow Flat Campground (12 sites, no water) is often full. Four-wheel driving along designated roads, including White Rim Trail in the Island in the Sky and others in the Needles and the Maze. The Maze ranger station is 46 miles from the highway along a rough dirt road. Squaw Flat Campground (26 sites) in the Needles has water April through September. Primitive backcountry campsites for four-wheel-drive parties are available on a first come, first-served basis in the Needles and the Maze; backcountry vehicle sites for the White Rim should be reserved well in advance (by mail or in person only). State park campsites are located at Dead Horse Point near the Island in the Sky. Overnight backcountry permits required. Rafting, hiking, four-wheel driving, educational programs, mountain biking, and horseback tours are available from concessionaires in Moab and Green River year-round; concessionaire in Monticello offers white-water rafting and educational programs. Commercial campgrounds and full services are available in Moab, Monticello, and Green River. Services and supplies available seasonally at Needles Outpost. For more information, write: Superintendent, Canyonlands National Park, 2282 S. West Resource Blvd., Moab, UT 84532; or telephone (435) 259-7164. www.nps.gov/cany

The story of Canyonlands, like that of the Grand Canyon, is written in rock strata exposed by the erosive power of the Colorado and Green rivers. Three hundred million years ago, movements along ancient faults formed the Uncompahgre Uplift to the northeast. The Paradox Basin dropped down simultaneously in the area of the present park. Debris from the highlands washed into the basin, which had been inundated by numerous shallow seas. Between advances, the seawater evaporated, leaving the Paradox Formation—salt deposits thousands of feet thick. Seas, rivers, and tidal flats contributed more layers of silt, sand, mud, and the limy deposits from the shells of dying marine creatures. In time, these sediments fused into rock. Pressure from this overlying rock forced the Paradox salt layer to flow away from the overburden, resulting in the fracturing of the overlying sediments. The movement and dissolution of this underlying layer of salt together with relentless erosion are principally responsible for the visual drama of the Needles.

The Colorado and Green rivers have already cut through a vertical mile of sedimentary rock in the Canyonlands region, and no evidence remains of younger, eroded rocks. The rock strata visible at Canyonlands today are 2,000 feet thick, piled high like a club sandwich. The oldest, the Paradox and Honaker Trail formations, can be seen only in deep canyons. But Navajo Sandstone, the famous "slickrock" formed from Jurassic-age "petrified" sand dunes, caps the Island in the Sky. The pinkish-striped arches, fins, spires, and buttes populating the Needles and the pale labyrinth of the Maze generally consist of rocks of the Cutler Group, sheared into fantastically shaped columns by water eroding down vertical joints. Their dark streaks of "desert varnish" derive from iron and manganese oxides. Forming a distinctive ledge above the tortuous river canyons is the White Rim Sandstone, visible from the Island in the Sky and along the 100-mile-long, four-wheel-drive White Rim Trail. The sloping Moenkopi and Chinle formations take a giant step back from the rim

Fragile microbiotic crust.

Fremont pictographs, Horseshoe Canyon.

View from the Maze Overlook.

here, meeting the vertiginous Wingate and Kayenta cliffs with their erosion-resistant Navajo Sandstone top layer.

Canyonlands received little attention from whites until Major John Wesley Powell surveyed the Green and Colorado rivers in 1869 and 1871–1872. But he was by no means the first person to enter this inhospitable region. Paleo-hunters had chased large animals through here 10,000 years before, when the climate was cooler and moister. Next came groups of Archaic hunter-gatherers who wandered the area and left behind striking pictographs and petroglyphs in the Great Gallery in isolated Horseshoe Canyon and elsewhere. Then, about 2,000 years ago, agriculture made its way into this marginal land, and small family groups began to cultivate maize, beans, and squash to supplement their traditional diet. These people, who came to be known by the Navajo name of Anasazi, or "Ancient Ones," developed a culture that, at its height around A.D. 1000 to 1200, consisted of communal living in multiroomed structures, agriculture and hunting and gathering, and fine crafts. Others among these talented people constructed Mesa Verde's lofty cliff pueblos, but here the structures were scaled down into less complex groups of dwellings. The Anasazi shared this land with the less-understood, hunter-gatherer Fremont who lived to the north and west.

Migrant Navajo and Ute Indians followed Anasazi and Fremont tenure, but not until 1836 did an Anglo, fur trapper Denis Julien, leave his mark in the canyonlands. Miners panned for gold on the Colorado in the late 1800s, and large ranching operations brought horses and cattle into the canyons, each group contributing names like Gold Bar Canyon and Grays Pasture. In the fifties, uranium deposits in the Chinle Formation drew prospectors; the Shafer Trail in the Island in the Sky, originally a cattle trail, was employed again during this boom.

Elevations at Canyonlands generally range between 4,000 and 6,000 feet, although Cedar Mesa in the Needles District is nearly 7,000 feet high. The diverse landscape allows varied plants and animals to survive here, despite desert conditions. Coyotes, foxes, and squirrels inhabit the lower reaches, while ravens, hawks, falcons, and eagles patrol the skies. In between, rare desert bighorn sheep are sometimes seen on the White Rim. Water brings the desert to life. Preternaturally green cottonwoods and tamarisks line the river banks, and hanging gardens of maidenhair fern and columbine form thick clusters at seeps. Look for bobcats, beavers, deer, birds, and other small animals that often visit these reliable water sources.

Canyonlands became a national park in 1964 through the committed work of Secretary of the Interior Stewart Udall, U.S. Senator Frank Moss, and Superintendent Bates Wilson of what was then Arches National Monument. Further expanded in 1971, Canyonlands preserves a remarkable desert landscape and is one of our most striking national parks.

Molar Rock and Angel Arch in The Needles.

Chesler Park, The Needles.

Tower Ruin, The Needles.

Cottonwood in Horse Canyon, The Maze.

CAPITOL REEF NATIONAL PARK

VISITOR INFORMATION

378 sq. mi. Entrance fee. Open year-round; spring, fall, and winter best times, summers may be hot. Visitor center open 8 A.M. to 4:30 P.M. daily, extended hours in summer; information, exhibits, summer interpretive programs. Historic and geologic sites in Fruita; 20-mile round-trip scenic drive from Highway 24; four-wheel-drive necessary on north roads in the park. Backcountry hiking on trails recommended off-season. Take plenty of water and wear a hat; this is the desert. 71 campsites at Fruita campground available on first-come, first-served basis; backcountry camping allowed in much of park by permit. Campgrounds in Dixie and Fishlake national forests. No food, lodging, or supplies available in park; come prepared. Small nearby towns have facilities. For more information, write: Superintendent, Capitol Reef National Park, Torrey, UT 84775; or telephone (435) 425-3791. www.nps.gov/care

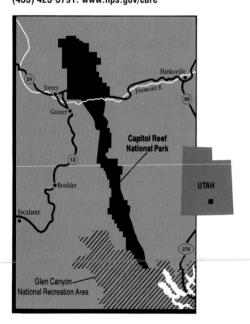

Fremont petroglyphs.

Chimney Rock.

Local boosters in the 1920s dubbed Utah's startling Capitol Reef "Wayne Wonderland" (for its location in Wayne County). To the Navajo, it was the "Land of the Sleeping Rainbow." We know it today as Capitol Reef National Park, encompassing much of the 100-mile-long Waterpocket Fold—a spectacular, weather-sculpted warp in the earth's surface that splits the south-central area of the state in two. The Fold was named by early travelers for pockets in the rocks that fill with life-giving water during rainstorms. Capitol Reef itself is an especially scenic, ten-mile-long section of the Fold just south of the Fremont River, so-named by fanciful explorers because its high rocky ramparts seemed like an impossible ocean reef and its smooth domes were reminiscent of the U.S. Capitol in Washington.

Located halfway between Bryce Canyon and Canyonlands national parks, this desert park's 378 square miles highlight stratified rock formations, made all the more fascinating by a host of desert plants and animals and the remains of 1,200 years of human enterprise. Whether you sightsee from Highway 24, which crosses the park east to west paralleling the Fremont River, explore Indian shelters and the old Mormon settlement of Fruita, take the twenty-mile scenic drive, hike on designated trails, four-wheel drive on dirt roads, or roam the backcountry, you will be rewarded for your closer inspection of Capitol Reef.

The ridges and troughs of Cathedral Valley parallel the northeast exposure of the Waterpocket Fold, revealing much about the geologic forces that created the Fold. Accessible only by four-wheel-drive roads or on foot, 500-foot monoliths of reddish Entrada Sandstone distinguish this silent, highly eroded landscape. Brush-covered flats to the east contrast with lonely cathedral spires. Animals retreat to cool canyons, water sources, and burrows to escape daytime heat, with most emerging at night. Life exists—but very quietly.

Scientists believe that massive earth movements along and beneath the California coast 65 million years ago ultimately gave birth to Capitol Reef's convoluted geography. This period of intense mountain building, known as the Laramide Orogeny, apparently reverberated eastward, squeezing the many layers of sedimentary rocks that had accumulated following millennia of inundation by seas, rivers, tidal flats, and sand dunes. A series of steep, north-south–oriented monoclines, or folds, resulted; one of the most spectacular examples is the Waterpocket Fold. Later volcanic activity also reworked the landscape. Laccolithic mountains like the Henrys were created by deep, molten rock that intruded and pushed up overlying sedimentary strata. Lava surfaced along other faults and helped create the massif of Thousand Lake Mountain to the north. Much later, glaciers ground and crushed igneous rock that was once lava.

The Colorado Plateau was lifted above sea level, and forces of erosion began to carve the cliffs, spires, natural bridges, arches, and hogbacks of Capitol Reef. Along the southern section of the Waterpocket Fold, which reaches south to Bullfrog Basin at Lake Powell, kaleidoscopic bands of sandstone roll in 1,500-foot waves down to the valley floor. Domes cap the Fold, and natural arches and bridges formed by wind and water may be admired here. The "Escarpment" section of Capitol Reef towering over the scenic drive, displays red Wingate Sandstone topped with creamy Navajo Sandstone.

The winding Fremont River, named after explorer John C. Fremont who crossed its headwaters in 1853, has assured life here. Supplementing the scant eight inches of annual rainfall received locally, the river supports myriad plants and animals and provided irrigation for Indian farmers between A.D. 700 and 1275. It was no less important to nineteenth-century Mormon pioneers. Indeed, the vital green of tamarisk, cottonwood, willow, and box elder, along with Fruita's fruit orchards, haunt the memory long after leaving Capitol Reef.

Although the Waterpocket Fold presented a daunting barrier to travelers, some found paths through its canyons. Desert creatures like the ringtail, coyote, jackrabbit, and gray fox knew its byways, as eventually did a group of Archaic Desert people who apparently hunted and gathered throughout the region. Later, some Native Americans began to cultivate maize here to supplement their diet of game and wild crops. By A.D. 700, they were installed at Capitol Reef, living in pit houses, building stone granaries in caves to store their strain of hardy maize, and eventually adding beans and squash to their crops. This group seems to have been distinct from the Anasazi, who lived farther south. Archeologists named them the Fremont culture, after the river flowing through their homeland.

The Fremont people remained pit house dwellers long after the Anasazi were constructing aboveground pueblos. They continued to rely more on hunting and gathering, and made hide moccasins with heels fashioned from a deer's dewclaw, unknown elsewhere. Distinctive, unpainted black or gray pottery with raised or tooled surfaces was an early trademark. Later, they began to fashion grayware painted black—similar to Mesa Verde ceramics—perhaps as a result of contact with the Anasazi. Clay figurines may have been used in rituals. Most unusual of all, however, was their rock art. Throughout some canyons they drew and pecked into rock huge trapezoidal human figures, often adorned with shields and jewelry and accompanied by bighorn sheep and other life forms.

In the thirteenth century, the Fremont left these watered valleys. The frustrations of subsistence farming during an unusually long drought, pressure from the encroaching Shoshonean culture, and overuse of resources likely led to the exodus. Perhaps the Fremont people joined hunter-gatherer Paiutes who were entering the area, or mingled with other cultures farther removed, then lost their identity as a people. No one really knows.

For centuries, Paiutes and Utes hunted and gathered in Capitol Reef. Then, following the reports of prospectors and cattlemen, a few Mormon families established the settlement of Junction (later Fruita) by the Fremont River in the 1880s. They planted orchards and supplied transient prospectors, cowboys, and occasionally desperadoes like Butch Cassidy's Wild Bunch, with fruit and supplies. The last residents left in the 1960s. Today, you can pick fruit at these well-maintained historic orchards. Also at Fruita is an old schoolhouse, the National Park Service visitor center, and a campground.

Narrowleaf yucca and Indian paintbush.

The Henry Mountains seen from the Burr Trail.

Fruita schoolhouse, ca. 1884.

The Fremont River.

CAPULIN VOLCANO
NATIONAL MONUMENT

*Capulin Volcano,
north view.*

VISITOR INFORMATION

1.2 sq. mi. Open year-round; spring through fall best. Visitor center open 8 A.M. to 4 P.M., longer in summer; information, audiovisual and interpretive programs, exhibits, bookstore. Hiking one-mile Crater Rim Trail recommended. Picnicking but no other facilities available. Nearest services and campground in Capulin. For more information, write: Superintendent, Capulin Volcano National Monument, Capulin, NM 88414; or telephone (505) 278-2201. www.nps.gov/capu

Sometime between 8,000 and 2,500 years ago, Folsom Man may have been startled while out hunting buffalo on the plains close to present-day Capulin by a sudden, roaring earthquake close to his encampment. As the sky grew as black as night, the air thick with a choking blanket of cinders and ash, a glow filled the sky to the south. Fearing for his life, this early ancestor abandoned the hunt and fled to safety, far from this nightmarish scene.

If he stayed nearby, he would have witnessed a remarkable sight after the clouds of debris had parted. Where once there had been flat, grassy land, there was now a towering cone of dark, smoldering cinders a thousand feet high, belching smoke from a 415-foot-deep crater. The ground still quivered with earthquakes, as this newcomer and other nearby volcanoes grew along geologic faults, reshaping the land in what is now northeastern New Mexico. Capulin Volcano was born.

As the gases inside the volcano cooled, lava oozed copiously from its western flank, each flow building on the last—sometimes blocky and fast-flowing, other times viscous and ropy. Eventually, terraces of black lava rock extended from the base of the cone. In time, the lava ceased flowing; when it had completely cooled, hardy lichens were gradually able to colonize the steep sides of the

new mountain, breaking down lava into soil and providing a base for a few slow-growing, stunted pinyon and juniper trees, Gambel oak, and mountain mahogany. Squirrels set up housekeeping in the tree trunks, chipmunks scampered among the rocks, and mule deer munched on abundant grass and bushes. Hardy Indian paintbrush, daisies, lupines, and bluebells again brightened the vast plains with a rainbow of color every summer.

Indians used Capulin Volcano as a landmark on their travels, as did later Spanish conquistadors, who named the mountain "Capulin," after the tasty chokecherry growing abundantly on its slopes. In the nineteenth century, the volcano served as a beacon to American travelers coming west on the arduous Cimarron Cutoff section of the Santa Fe Trail.

All is now tranquility at Capulin Volcano. Since 1916, this classic cinder cone has been a national monument, attracting visitors who hike along the one-mile Crater Rim Trail, study the different lava forms, and, from the summit, enjoy views of Oklahoma, Colorado, Texas, and the snowcapped Sangre de Cristo Mountains to the west. A film about a volcanic event in Mexico in 1943, similar to that which built Capulin, is shown in the visitor center, offering an insight into this region's volcanic origins. Those familiar with El Malpais National Monument near Grants, New Mexico, which began to erupt around the same time as Capulin, will gain a further appreciation for the restless geology of the region.

*Mountain mahogany
and lichens.*

CARLSBAD CAVERNS NATIONAL PARK

The Big Room,
Carlsbad Cavern.

VISITOR INFORMATION

Approximately 73 sq. mi. Entrance fee. Open year-round, except Christmas Day, 8 A.M. to 5:30 P.M. (winter), 8 A.M. to 7 P.M. (summer). Visitor center: audiovisual program, interpretive activities, information, exhibits, bookstore, gift shop, restaurant, kennel, day care center. 2 different tours of cavern; last tours 3:30 P.M. winter, 5 P.M. summer. For safety reasons, first part of Blue Tour is ranger-led in winter. Radio tour guides may be rented for a small fee. Lunchroom and restrooms available within cavern and next to visitor center. Ranger-led tour of undeveloped Slaughter Canyon Cave by reservation, call 1-800-967-CAVE; recommended for physically fit only—wear sturdy shoes and bring flashlight and water. Bat flights preceded by ranger talks nightly (May to October only). 9.5-mile Walnut Canyon Desert Drive offers one-way scenic loop through Guadalupe Mountains (not suitable for trailers or motorhomes). 50 miles of backcountry hikes; hikers must register first. Temperatures vary in desert mountains; come prepared. A good topographical map and adequate water are essential. No camping in park, but picnicking areas available at visitor center and Rattlesnake Springs (a detached area of park). Campgrounds and other services in nearby Whites City and Carlsbad. For more information, write: Superintendent, Carlsbad Caverns National Park, 3225 National Parks HIghway, Carlsbad, NM 88220; or telephone (505) 785-2232. www.nps.gov/cave

Deep beneath the beautiful Guadalupe Mountains near the New Mexico–Texas border are some of nature's strangest and most spectacular art works. Within the dark netherworld of Carlsbad Caverns, curious, precipitated, crystalline formations crowd the dripping surfaces of enormous subterranean chambers like courtiers in "The Hall of the Mountain King." Their translucent shapes are continually evolving: some are enormous, dominating an entire room; some remain small and delicate, like frozen icicles.

There is much to do above ground in Carlsbad Caverns National Park, from hiking desert mountains to photographing unique wildlife. But the highlight for most people is the descent into Carlsbad Cavern to view the remarkable mineral deposits and corridors that eventually lead to the Big Room, one of the largest underground chambers in the world.

The limestone rock in which the park's many caverns formed was originally a 400-mile-long, horseshoe-shaped reef, which grew along an offshore shelf of an inland sea 250 million years ago. The reef was composed of lime precipitated from the sea water, and limy secretions from sponges and calcareous algae. Eventually this ancient sea became landlocked and evaporated, causing the reef to be covered by salt, gypsum, potash, and other sedimentary deposits. Then, about 10 million years ago, geologic uplift in the region gave birth to the Guadalupe Range, once again exposing parts of the fossil reef. The young mountains were particularly vulnerable to rain-

water acidified by carbon dioxide from decaying organic material and the atmosphere. This solution mixed with organic matter in the soil and permeated surface cracks in the limestone, gradually dissolving the rock until large caves were hollowed out within the mountains. Some scientists now believe that fresh water, mixed with hydrogen-sulfide gas seeping into the reef from the oil-rich basin to the south, produced sulfuric acid and accelerated corrosion of the limestone.

The features in Carlsbad Cavern, the largest cave in the park, may have begun forming about 500,000 years ago. A wetter, cooler climate intensified seepage into the underground chambers, where carbon dioxide loss from water droplets and evaporation left behind calcite crystal formations.

(continued)

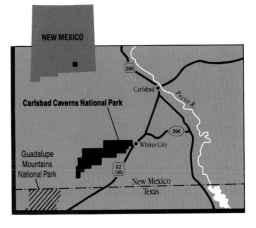

The natural entrance
to Carlsbad Cavern.

The Christmas Tree, New Cave.

Mexican free-tailed bat.

Lake of the Clouds, Carlsbad Cavern.

The Chandelier Ballroom, Lechuguilla Cave.

MICHAEL NICHOLS/MAGNUM

SCOTT ALTENBACH

DAVID JAGNOW

MICHAEL NICHOLS/MAGNUM

In the Hall of Giants, formations like Twin Domes are actually enormous stalagmites growing up from the floor. In other places, stalactites hang from the ceiling in great numbers and, where stalactites and stalagmites meet, great columns have grown up. Smaller iciclelike stalactites called soda straws hang in curtains, while eccentric helictites amazingly seem to grow in all directions. Smooth flowstone covers many sloping surfaces with marblelike deposits and, in places, slow-moving water has caused rimstone dams to form. Water is a constant here, forming pools and lakes that may eventually become obscured by calcite lily pads. Rarely, one may see delicate, needlelike aragonite formations, a product of similar depositional processes but with a different crystalline structure.

Visitors descend into Carlsbad Cavern on foot via the 3-mile Blue Tour, or into the 750-foot-deep Big Room by elevator on the 1.25-mile Red Tour. The longer tour begins at the large natural entrance to the cavern and descends steeply through the Main Corridor to the Green Lake Room, Kings Palace, Queens Chamber, and Papoose Room, which make up the exquisitely decorated Scenic Rooms. The spectacular Big Room is located just beyond the Boneyard. Rangers are stationed throughout the cavern, and talks are given periodically at the Top of the Cross in the Big Room. More caves, similarly decorated, continue to be found by experienced cavers. There are now seventy-five known caves at Carlsbad. More adventurous and physically fit visitors may wish to take the tour of New Cave, discovered in 1937, which offers a primitive caving experience in an undeveloped area of the park.

Carlsbad Cavern is well known for another fascinating natural phenomenon. More than 300,000 Mexican free-tailed bats raise their young in the Bat Cave passage in spring and summer months. During the day, the small, leathery-winged bats sleep upside down, hanging from the ceiling of Bat Cave; the young are born here in June. At dusk the parents awake and hunt for insects, exiting the main entrance of the cavern in a thick, black swarm—a nightly spectacle that can continue from twenty minutes to several hours. Bats track food and avoid obstacles by emitting high-frequency sound waves that bounce off objects around them. At dawn, their return to the cave is equally mesmerizing. As each bat arrives home, it plummets into the darkness with folded wings that create a strange buzzing sound. These bat flights may be viewed from a seating area near the cave entrance and are a remarkable experience that should not be missed.

The caves were used by Indians perhaps as long as 12,000 years ago, who left behind paintings that signal their passage. But not until cowboy Jim White stumbled upon Carlsbad Cavern at the turn of the century did this unique geology become widely known. White was attracted by large deposits of bat droppings known as guano, which make excellent fertilizer; soon, though, he was crowing about an even greater find—the scenic caves. To prove his strange tales, White had a friend take photographs of the decorated underground rooms, which created a stir when they were exhibited in the town of Carlsbad in 1915. White soon found himself giving tours of the undeveloped cavern, unceremoniously using a guano bucket to lower visitors below. As a result of public enthusiasm, the cave was designated a national monument in 1923, with White named chief ranger. Carlsbad Cavern became a national park in 1930 and has provided extraordinary memories for millions ever since.

CASA GRANDE RUINS NATIONAL MONUMENT

Casa Grande Ruins National Monument is the only site in the national park system devoted to the prehistoric desert farmers known as the Hohokam, Piman for "those who have gone." Beginning around A.D. 200 to 500 and ending in approximately 1450, these Sonoran Desert dwellers lived communally and produced distinctive arts and crafts. According to recent evidence, they may have been among the first North Americans to perfect sophisticated irrigated farming.

The group of partially excavated prehistoric structures here once formed a village, surrounded by a high wall. Entry to the compounds and to many of the dwellings within was afforded by ladders, although a north entrance to the village existed. The village's central focus remains the four-story Casa Grande, or "Great House," ruin, whose function remains a mystery to archeologists. The structure looks out onto terraced fields that once supported corn, squash, beans, and cotton. To supplement their diet, the Hohokam also hunted small game and rodents, fished and dug for clams in the Gila River, and collected cactus fruits and seeds. Their farmlands were once linked by a 600-mile network of narrow irrigation canals leading from the Gila two miles away. This method of irrigation, found throughout ancient Meso-america, is generally considered the Hohokam's greatest achievement and allowed them to farm the arid desert for many centuries. But depletion of the soil from extensive irrigation, along with climatic changes and flooding, may have contributed to the final disappearance of the Hohokam culture.

Casa Grande was first seen by Europeans when Father Eusebio Kino, a Jesuit missionary, visited in 1694; its tower has served as a landmark ever since. A series of archeological excavations, starting in 1891 and continuing until the 1970s, has uncovered myriad clues about the Great House, but agreement as to its origin and exact use has never been reached. It was apparently built quite late—in the early 1300s—using caliche mud, made from the limy desert subsoil. Such structures supplanted the mud-and-wood houses previously built by the Hohokam.

Although cleared now, the first story of Casa Grande was originally filled with five feet of dirt, necessitating entry by ladder to the second story. This and the third level had five rooms each, with just one large room on the fourth floor that may have been surrounded by a low parapet. The structure has massive walls that taper to the top on the outside to reduce weight on the foundation. Scientists suggest that Casa Grande perhaps served as a residence for important leaders. Or it may have been used as an astronomical lookout; the existence of holes in the walls that admit sunlight

Casa Grande Ruin with modern protective roof.

on the equinox and solstices, and the demonstrated interest of Central American cultures in astronomy, give some weight to this idea. Strong Mesoamerican influence is also felt in the presence of a late-period, walled ball court—probably used for ceremonial gatherings and ball games—along with features called platform mounds.

In the 1200s, most likely as a result of interaction with northern cultures, the Hohokam began to make attractive polychromatic ceramics that surpassed their more basic red-on-buff pottery. Already skilled toolmakers and renowned shell etchers, they also turned to making beautiful jewelry from bartered shells and turquoise.

Were these people originally part of the more advanced cultures of Mesoamerica, or were they Desert Archaic hunter-gatherers who gradually absorbed information from the south? We shall probably never know because the Hohokam ceased to be a cultural entity after the early 1400s, and their likely descendants, the Pima, reverted to a largely hunter-gatherer existence in the surrounding region. The mystery of the Hohokam continues to intrigue today.

VISITOR INFORMATION

472 acres. Entrance fee. Open 8 A.M. to 5 P.M. year-round. Visitor center: exhibits, information, bookstore. 400-yard self-guided trail through ruins; 45-minute ranger-led tours are also given throughout the day. Summers are very hot and often wet. A picnic area is provided, but nearest lodging, camping, and services are in Coolidge, 1 mile away. For more information, write: Superintendent, Casa Grande Ruins National Monument, 1100 Ruins Drive, Coolidge, AZ 85228; or telephone (520) 723-3172. www.nps.gov/cagr

Hohokam red-on-buff pot, A.D. 1100.

CEDAR BREAKS
NATIONAL MONUMENT

The Cedar Breaks Amphitheater.

Orange sneezeweed, lupine, Indian paintbrush.

VISITOR INFORMATION

9.5 sq. mi. Entrance fee. Services and roads in this high country national monument usually open June to mid-October only, cross-country skiing and snowmobiling highly recommended in winter. National Park Service headquarters is at Kolob Visitor Center, Zion National Park (Exit 40, off I-15). On-site visitor center open summer 8 A.M. to 6 P.M., shorter hours in fall: information, interpretive services, and bookstore. 5-mile rim drive, 2 main hiking trails, and 1 backcountry trail. 30 National Park Service first-come, first-served campsites (June to September only), picnicking. Forest Service campsites and alpine resorts nearby. Superb scenic drive between Cedar Breaks and Bryce Canyon. No food, lodging, or services in monument. Nearest facilities in Brian's Head, Panguitch Lake, or Cedar City. For more information, write: Superintendent, Cedar Breaks National Monument, 82 North, 100 East, Suite #3, Cedar City, UT 84720; or telephone (801) 586-9451. www.nps.gov/cebr

Newcomers to the spectacular canyon country of southern Utah may be tempted to think of Cedar Breaks National Monument as just a smaller, quieter version of its nearby bigger relation, Bryce Canyon National Park. Certainly, both places share similar geological origins and lie within just a few hours of each other along one of the most scenic highways in the country. But Cedar Breaks, a three-mile-wide amphitheater of marvelously eroded, reddish limestone surrounded by fragrant alpine forests and meadows, more than holds its own. A side trip here, preferably in late June when the wildflowers are at their most beguiling, should be on every visitor's itinerary.

The unearthly, multihued rock formations that cluster along this western edge of the 10,000-foot-high Markagunt Plateau were probably a complete surprise to the nineteenth-century Mormon settlers who happened upon them, for only on drawing near the precipitous cliff edge does the gallery of spires, columns, arches, and canyons become eye-openingly apparent.

Early Indians referred to this masterpiece of nature as the Circle of Painted Cliffs. Mormon dairy farmers who settled in this part of Utah dubbed it Cedar Breaks: "cedar," the name for the hardy juniper tree, and "breaks" describing the rocky badlands. Nevertheless, only a few people were familiar with the area until 1933, when Cedar Breaks became a national monument.

Millennia of relentless erosion by rain, streams, ice, and wind have forged eerie hoodoos. These strangely eroded spires are made up of the rocks of the Claron Formation, the product of sediments laid down by ancient streams and lakes. These rocks are part of the Markagunt Plateau, which in turn is part of the Pink Cliffs, one of a series of cliffs uplifted about 15 million years ago in what is called the Grand Staircase. Near Cedar Breaks, lava and cinder cones associated with the

Brian Head Flow bear silent witness to earlier volcanic activity in this geologically active region.

Different perspectives on Cedar Breaks are afforded from the four scenic overlooks along the five-mile rim drive, and from two hiking trails. Readily apparent at this 10,300-foot elevation are dense forests of fir, quaking aspen, and Engelmann spruce, which shelter portions of the Alpine Pond Trail. But a special treat for hikers along the Wasatch Ramparts Trail is the stand of rare, thousand-year-old bristlecone pines growing at Spectra Point. Birds like the Clark's nutcracker and the acrobatic violet-green swallow are frequently encountered here, sharing these cool mountain heights with such earthbound denizens as pikas, marmots, squirrels, and mule deer, and, on rare occasions, the more reticent mountain lion. A floral extravaganza awaits summer visitors. Indian paintbrush, wild roses, shooting stars, penstemons, lupines, and other delicate wildflowers carpet the meadows in a rainbow of colors. But winter can be equally seductive in this peaceful high country environment. Growing in popularity are cross-country skiing, snowshoeing, and snowmobiling, although self-sufficiency is required as park facilities are closed at this time of year.

Tri-walled structure,
Pueblo del Arroyo.

VISITOR INFORMATION

Approximately 53 sq. mi. Entrance fee. Open year-round, ruins sunrise to sunset, visitor center 8 A.M. to 5 P.M. (to 6 P.M. between Memorial Day and Labor Day). Dirt roads into park can be difficult in bad weather; check locally before setting out. Visitor center: audiovisual program, exhibits, interpretive activities (including ranger-led tours of the ruins), information, bookstore. Hiking is best way to see the park. 5 self-guided trails lead through ruins and petroglyph sites; 4 backcountry trails reach more remote sites. Wijiji Trail is the only designated bicycle trail. All trails are closed from sunset to sunrise. At this 6,200-foot elevation, summers are warm and subject to rainstorms; winter days are pleasant with very cold nights. Gallo Campground has 51 campsites and picnic tables available on a first-come, first-served basis. Drinking water at visitor center only. Groups of 15 or more may reserve space in advance, except on summer holiday weekends. There are no visitor services, fuel wood, or gasoline in the park; come prepared. Supplies are available on NM Highway 44. Lodging and restaurants in Grants, Gallup, and Farmington. For more information, write: Superintendent, Chaco Culture National Historical Park, P.O. Box 220, Nageezi, NM 87037; or telephone (505) 786-7014. www.nps.gov/chcu

If there is a place in the United States where one feels the past crowding in, Chaco Canyon in northwestern New Mexico is it, for, in the A.D. 900s, this meditative, high desert landscape, with its lonely buttes and gathering silences, became the center for the powerful Anasazi civilization.

Chaco Canyon's sandstone walls were carved by an intermittent stream, which floods during the winter snowmelt and summer rains. Chaco Wash, a marginal oasis in this harsh, dry environment, attracts a tenacious population of water-loving plants and thirsty creatures. The remains of ancient spear tips, basketry, early pit house dwellings, and later masonry buildings suggest that Paleo-hunters, nomadic hunter-gatherers, Pueblo farmers, and modern Navajo herders have used this water source for at least 8,500 years. The first seasonal settlements at Chaco date back approximately 1,500 years, when Basketmaker Anasazi dug pit houses on the mesas and culti-vated squash, corn, and beans in mesa-top gardens and along Chaco Wash. These people supplemented their diet by consuming wild foods and hunting small game.

In the A.D. 700s, population growth and an expediency afforded by close-knit living may have led to the appearance of pueblos, which consisted of multiroomed, masonry dwellings built beside former pit houses that became ceremonial cham-bers called *kivas*. In the late 900s, advances in technology, the arts and sciences, and religious thought took place, and Chaco's influence was felt throughout the San Juan Basin. Great houses, probably used seasonally as community buildings, appeared. Today, the most dramatic evidence of Chaco's golden age is found in the well-preserved architecture of Pueblo Bonito, Chetro Ketl, Pueblo Arroyo, and Kin Kletso ruins.

The most complex of all these structures is Pueblo Bonito, a three-acre, D-shaped, planned great house built by many generations of Chacoan masons. It eventually rose five stories high in the back, dipping to one story in front, and contained more than 600 large rooms around a plaza dotted with three great kivas and more than thirty small ones. The walls are characterized by sandstone slabs chinked with smaller stones, which were apparently mud plastered and painted on com-pletion. Chacoan architects favored rubble core veneer masonry construction, a way of reinforcing structures by filling the space between two tapering, parallel walls with rubble and mortar. Massive amounts of timber from distant forests were used to make sturdy roofs and lintels over perfectly shaped doorways.

(continued)

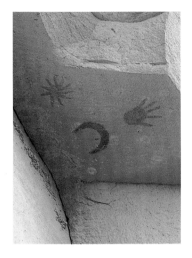

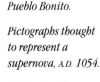

Pueblo Bonito.

Pictographs thought to represent a supernova, A.D. 1054.

Distinctive Chacoan masonry.

Doorways, Pueblo Bonito.

The presence of so many kivas in the canyon indicates their importance in daily Chacoan life. Casa Rinconada is one of the largest great kivas in the Southwest and may have been used for huge communal gatherings, ceremonies, education, and other functions serving to join the communities. In the 1930s, archeologist Gordon Vivian discovered many niches in kiva walls, where ceremonial offerings may have been placed. The location of the niches and other natural and architectural features throughout the canyon indicates that Chacoans may have been tracking astronomical events; some features were perhaps used as solstice markers, allowing priests to gauge when ceremonies should be performed. Near Casa Rinconada, steps carved into the canyon walls lead to strategically placed Tsin Kletsin, a mesa-top pueblo with a panoramic view of the horizon. A network of line-of-sight signaling stations along the mesa tops was also apparently used for communication.

Current evidence strongly points to Chaco having been a spiritual and operational center for the entire San Juan region. Researchers have discovered hundred of miles of prehistoric roads tied into a system that centers in Chaco. Road segments are found at most of the great house buildings scattered throughout the San Juan basin,

and a forty-mile-long segment extends from the canyon due north to the San Juan River area. While the wide, straight roads may have been used for transporting resources such as timber or food from one community to another, they may have had a more symbolic role in tying the region together. Chaco, with limited resources, may have relied on trading precious turquoise for food, pottery, and other artifacts. New trade goods and ideas undoubtedly accompanied the mobile population, as evidenced by the copper bells, macaws, and architectural details such as the Mexican-style colonnade at enormous Chetro Ketl pueblo and later, the northern-style, tri-walled structure at Pueblo del Arroyo.

Archeologists originally conjectured that Chaco supported up to 6,000 people; however, a surprisingly small number of fireplaces, mealing bins, and burials, coupled with unusually large amounts of broken pottery indicating ceremonial usage, lead some to suspect that Chaco's year-round population may have been a small elite. Despite the extensive use of irrigation canals and other water control devices to direct rainwater from mesa top to canyon floor, a particularly long drought in the mid A.D. 1100s made life in Chaco Canyon too difficult. Chacoans slowly began to join pueblos on and between the Rio Grande and Little Colorado River drainages, where their descendants remain today.

By the mid-1200s, Chaco was scarcely used, save for a short occupation by Mesa Verde Anasazi; it was completely abandoned by that century's end. A group of hunter-gatherer Athapascans known as the Navajo arrived shortly thereafter in the region and, after learning herding from the Spaniards, began to inhabit Chaco Canyon. The Navajo still live here today, raising sheep and goats, selling excellent handicrafts, and working cash jobs on and off their large reservation. In the 1600s, the Spanish unsuccessfully attempted to subdue Navajo raiding of neighboring villages, a task eventually achieved by United States rule in the mid-1800s. Military action against the Navajo led to Lieutenant James H. Simpson's discovery of Chaco Canyon in 1849, followed in 1877 by a U.S. Geological and Geographical survey of the site.

The first excavations at Chaco were carried out by the Hyde Exploring Expedition from 1896 to 1900. Its leader was Richard Wetherill, the first Anglo-American to publicize the cliff dwellings at Mesa Verde. In 1907, Chaco was designated a national monument, largely through the dedication of archeologist Edgar Lee Hewitt. Discovery of the many Chacoan outliers led, in 1980, to the monument being expanded and redesignated Chaco Culture National Historical Park.

Summer symphony concert.

VISITOR INFORMATION

55 acres. Open year-round, 8 A.M. to 5 P.M. in winter, longer hours in summer, and until 11 P.M. during special events. No entrance fee, but tickets are sold for some theater performances. Visitor center museum with historical exhibits, award-winning bilingual documentary film, information, travel desk, bookstore, temporary gallery, theater. Special cultural programs emphasize performing and graphic arts. Outdoor amphitheater used for music fesitvals, such as The Siglo de Oro (Golden Age) Spanish Classical Drama Festival in March, the El Paso Jazz Festival in May, the El Paso/Zarzuela Festival in July and August, the Border Folk Music Festival in October, as well as national holiday celebrations. Mexican-style rodeos in special adjoining arena. Memorial is within walking distance of southern El Paso. Parking available. Picnicking permitted, but no camping. Lodging and other visitor facilities in El Paso and Ciudad Juárez. The land transferred to Mexico under the Chamizal Convention now includes 760-acre Chamizal Federal Park, which has an outstanding archeological museum and impressive monuments and sport facilities. For more information, write: Superintendent, Chamizal National Memorial, 800 San Marcial, El Paso, TX 79905; or telephone (915) 532-7273. www.nps.gov/cham

The Treaty of Guadalupe Hidalgo, which ended the United States War with Mexico in 1848, created a new boundary between the two nations. To survey, mark, and map this line, the treaty provided for an International Boundary Commission, with representatives from each nation. For eight years, from 1849 to 1857, the two sections of the first commission surveyed across almost 2,000 miles of rivers, deserts, and arid mountains.

The deepest channels of the Colorado River and the Rio Grande marked two-thirds of the boundary, and both rivers changed their courses with almost every flood season. The parcels of land affected by the river changes were called *bancos*, and in 1884, the principles for settling problems of banco nationality were agreed upon. The piece of land called Chamizal (named after the river thicket plants that grew there in the 1800s) was one such banco and would cause lawmakers more problems than any other disputed border territory.

In 1889, a second International Boundary Commission (IB&WC) was formed, following the pattern of the 1849 survey, and in 1906 was given broad authority to take action on bancos. But the Chamizal banco problem was not resolved. The boundary separating El Paso, Texas, and Ciudad Juárez, Mexico, was the Rio Grande, which meandered across its floodplain, changing a little almost every year. International agreement was reached on the boundary line in 1853, but by the 1860s the river had shifted south, and the first claims for settlement were made.

Maps of the critical period did not exist, and the method of the river's movement did not seem to fit the principles agreed upon for settling disputes. For almost a century, as questions of ownership slowed the growth of El Paso and Ciudad Juárez, the arguments continued. Compromise efforts failed in 1911 and 1930, and by 1961, the problem of the Chamizal was viewed by both nations as the greatest single barrier to closer cooperation.

In 1962, Presidents John F. Kennedy and Lopez Mateos met to resolve the dispute. A year later, the Chamizal Convention was legally approved by both nations, equitably dividing the disputed area and authorizing artificial shaping of the river bed to avoid future floods. The IB&WC, by 1944 supported by seven treaties, today manages flood control, irrigation, and legal matters related to the boundary. It is an example to the world in international cooperation.

Chamizal National Memorial was authorized in 1966 to commemorate the diplomatic triumph in resolving the Chamizal banco dispute and the history of the border country, including its occasional periods of sharp disagreement between neighbors whose languages and backgrounds differ. Despite these disagreements, border residents have maintained close relationships.

The memorial includes a small museum, a temporary display gallery, and indoor and outdoor performing art areas. The regular presentation of well-attended art displays and performances plays an integral role in furthering intercultural understanding.

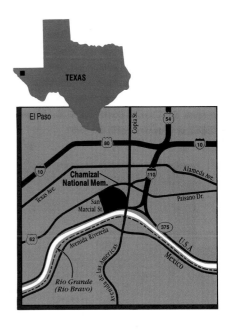

CHIRICAHUA NATIONAL MONUMENT

*Standing rocks along
Echo Canyon Trail.*

VISITOR INFORMATION

17 sq. mi. Entrance fee. Visitor center open 8 A.M. to 5 P.M. daily, except Christmas Day: audiovisual program, interpretive activities, exhibits, information, bookstore. 8-mile scenic drive with pullouts ends at Massai Point. 20 miles of maintained and unmaintained day use hiking trails. 3 self-guiding trails interpreting geology, natural history, and human history, and 1 discovery nature trail. Shuttle to main trailheads every morning. Summers are hot and can be wet. Bonita Canyon Campground near visitor center operates on first-come, first-served basis and has 26 campsites and picnic area. Campgrounds in Coronado National Forest to south. No services at monument; nearest gas, food, and lodging in nearby Willcox. For more information, write: Superintendent, Chiricahua National Monument, Dos Cabezas Route, Box 6500, Willcox, AZ 85643; or telephone (520) 824-3560. www.nps.gov/chir

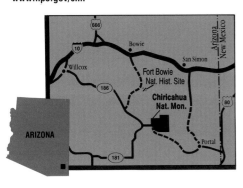

I hate to die and leave this place.
—Emma Erickson
Homesteader, Faraway Ranch

Blessed with a range of habitats from desert grassland to mountain forest, southeastern Arizona's Chiricahua National Monument is a pleasant refuge, providing shelter from the intensity of the surrounding Chihuahuan and Sonoran deserts. The natural beauty of the Chiricahua Mountains and the diverse wildlife here are not the only attractions, though. These mountains were set aside because of an outstanding collection of bizarre, eroded rocks in their midst. With forms and names as exotic as any plant or creature living here, Chiricahua's galleries of towering spires, pinnacles, pedestals, and huge balancing rocks are an inspiring sight.

Scientists believe that 25 million years ago, a massive volcanic eruption from neighboring Turkey Creek caldera spewed white-hot ash over this region. As the ash cooled, it fused into a 2,000-foot layer of rhyolite tuff; this dark volcanic rock provided the foundation for the Chiricahua Mountains, which arose during a later period of uplift. As a result of these turbulent beginnings, the new range was crisscrossed with many areas of weakness that presented perfect avenues for extensive sculpting by wind, water, and ice. These are the elements that have fashioned the "Land of Standing-Up Rocks," as the Chiricahua Apache called the extraordinary rockscape. Fancifully

named formations, including Duck on a Rock, Totem Pole, and Big Balanced Rock, can be found in the Heart of Rocks, seen best from the Massai Point Trail at the end of the eight-mile Bonita Canyon scenic drive.

A natural corridor running through the Chiricahuas to Mexico has attracted unusual wildlife, including many Mexican plants and animals that, oblivious to national borders, have made their homes here. Rare Apache fox squirrels and Chihuahua and Apache pines live happily alongside plants and animals typical of the Sonoran and Chihuahuan deserts. Nowhere else in this country can so many Mexican species of wildlife be found.

Because of the 5,160- to 7,365-foot elevation range, several life zones are found within the monument. Desert lowlands are home to cacti and scrub and creatures, such as kangaroo rats, coatimundis, collared peccaries, lizards, and snakes. An astonishing variety of birds, such as colorful sulphur-bellied flycatchers and chickadees live here, making birding a popular activity at Chiricahua. Forests of pinyon, alligator juniper, and Arizona cypress grow in shaded canyons. Rhyolite Canyon Trail leads visitors through a canyon riparian environment, a cool habitat for many desert dwellers. On exposed ridges, hardy manzanita, buckthorn, and skunkbush prosper, providing shade for rarely seen coral snakes, rattlesnakes, and lizards. Mountain slopes support lush forests of ponderosa pine, aspen, and Douglas fir that shut out the blazing sun, and wildflowers grow profusely here in spring and summer. Rich volcanic soil, adequate moisture, and cool temperatures make the high country a popular haunt for browsing white-tail deer and wide-ranging hunters, such as coyotes and bobcats, which make frequent excursions to these pleasant heights in search of food.

Fiercely independent Chiricahua Apaches lived in these sheltered canyons for centuries. Increasing encroachment on Apache lands by nineteenth-century American settlers resulted in the Indian Wars of the 1880s. A treaty eventually brought peace in 1886. Since then, few people have been lucky enough to know the splendid Chiricahua Mountains as well as the Erickson family. For close to ninety years, members of this pioneering Swedish family ran an isolated cattle ranch in Bonita Canyon. It was largely through their enthusiasm and tireless promotion that Chiricahua became a national monument in 1924. In 1988, one hundred years after they first moved into it, the Ericksons' Faraway Ranch came under the protection of the National Park Service. A trail leads to the ranch from the visitor center.

The first important European contact with North America was made by Spaniards, who explored and laid claim to vast areas of the American Southeast and Southwest between 1539 and 1542. One of the important expeditions charting the new lands was led by a charismatic, thirty-year-old Spaniard named Don Francisco Vásquez de Coronado. Coronado's fruitless, two-year search for the fabled gold of the Seven Cities of Cíbola took him from Compostela, Mexico, to present-day Kansas, across deserts, mountains, rivers, and plains dotted with Indian settlements. This important period in American history is highlighted today at Coronado National Memorial in the beautiful San Pedro River Valley on the Mexican border, where some believe Coronado first set foot on North American soil.

In 1536, survivors of an ill-fated expedition to Florida straggled into Mexico City after an eight-year trek from the Texas coast, telling stories of great cities to the north bursting with treasure. Two years later, Fray Marcos de Niza and one of the survivors, a Moor named Estéban, were sent north to verify these accounts. Fray Marcos returned to Mexico after Estéban was slain in Cíbola, the Spanish name for seven of the Indian pueblos of the Zuni. Based on the priest's favorable reports, Coronado, accompanied by 336 well-equipped soldiers, 1,000 Indians, 4 priests, and 3 women, set out in February 1540 from Compostela toward this new El Dorado.

In June, after months of torrid desert temperatures, Coronado's party may have passed within sight of 6,864-foot Coronado Peak in the present-day memorial. The expedition probably followed well-trodden Indian trading trails all the way to Cíbola, through the almost-impassable Gila Mountains and the *despoblado*, or "unpopulated land," crossing the Gila, Black, and White rivers along the way. Coronado and his army encountered many friendly Indians, who presented them with food and gifts and taught them about the new land. But the dream of gold proved illusory. Upon entering the Zuni pueblo of Hawikuh, just east of the present Arizona–New Mexico border, the only treasure to be found was a handful of inferior gems.

Undaunted, Coronado pressed eastward to the Rio Grande, passing close to present-day El Morro National Monument, the Sky Pueblo of Acoma, and wintering at Tiguex Pueblo by present-day Bernalillo, New Mexico. The following April, the expedition continued northeastward to the great pueblo of Cicuyé, now Pecos National Historical Park, where Coronado believed the wild tales about gold on the northeastern plains told by a captive Plains Indian who the Spanish named

"The Turk." After months of weary travel through the Texas and Oklahoma panhandles, Coronado's party finally realized they had been duped and returned to Mexico.

The Spanish Crown considered the entire journey an expensive failure—despite the information it had yielded about the new territory—and hushed up the whole saga. Coronado and one of his men, García López de Cárdenas, were put on trial for their lives, narrowly beating conviction. Most of the expedition's participants died in poverty and obscurity, but later historians would deem the journey one of the milestones in Spain's colonial history.

Coronado National Memorial was established in 1952 and is the largest of twenty-eight memorials in the national park system. It is set amid grasslands and rugged, forested mountains that would still be recognizable to Coronado today. In addition to its historic interest, the area is popular with hikers and birders.

Black-chinned hummingbird.

View down Montezuma Canyon.

VISITOR INFORMATION

Approximately 4.5 sq. mi. No entrance fee. Open year-round. Visitor center: 8 A.M. to 5 P.M.; exhibits, information, interpretive activities, bookstore. Self-guided nature trails to Coronado Peak and in canyons. Climate is temperate year-round, although summers may be hot and rainy with some snow in winter. Picnicking allowed at memorial, but no camping. Closest campgrounds are in adjoining Coronado National Forest. Nearest large town is Sierra Vista, 22 miles away. Other sites interpreting the Coronado Trail are Pecos National Historical Park, Salinas Pueblo Missions National Monument, and Coronado State Monument—all in New Mexico. For more information, write: Superintendent, Coronado National Memorial, 4101 East Montezuma Canyon Road, Hereford, AZ 85615; or telephone (520) 366-5515. www.nps.gov/coro

CURECANTI
NATIONAL RECREATION AREA

Blue Mesa Lake.

VISITOR INFORMATION

63.3 sq. mi. Pleasant spring through fall; dress very warmly in winter. Elk Creek Visitor Center open mid-May to late September from 8 A.M. to 6 P.M. (call for off-season hours): information, audiovisual and interpretive programs, exhibits, bookstore. Hiking, birding, fishing, and water sports in general, but swimming not recommended. Cross-country skiing, snowshoeing, snowmobiling, and ice fishing in winter. Concessionaires operate tours of Morrow Point Lake and Morrow Point Dam powerplant (Memorial Day through Labor Day), marinas, services, boat rentals, and horseback rides. Narrow-gauge railroad exhibit at Cimarron. 342 campsites in 4 main campgrounds and 44 campsites in 5 smaller grounds; 2 group sites accommodating a total of 50 people, by reservation only. No camping outside designated campgrounds. For more information, write: Superintendent, Curecanti National Recreation Area, 102 Elk Creek, Gunnison, CO 81230; or telephone (970) 641-2337. www.nps.gov/cure

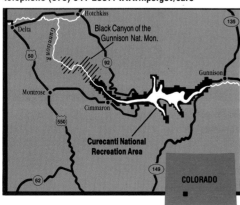

These days humans are frequent visitors. Water activities, along with hiking, camping, and birdwatching, provide recreational opportunities aplenty in the surrounding Curecanti National Recreation Area, named in honor of Ute Indian Chief Curicata. Although water sports, such as power boating, sailing, waterskiing, and windsurfing, are big attractions on twenty-mile-long Blue Mesa Lake, fishing is the principal draw here.

There are many wonderful hiking trails and campsites in the recreation area from which to choose. Be aware that this is steep canyon country—rapid elevation gains of up to 1,000 feet occur on some trails. Nevertheless, hikes are available here for all abilities: from the level riparian environment of 1.5-mile Neversink Trail to the six-mile challenge of steep Hermit's Rest Trail. In winter, ice fishing, cross-country skiing, and snowmobiling are popular activities, but come well prepared—temperatures can dip to forty degrees below zero, worsened by strong winds. The chance to see bald eagles and herds of deer and elk makes a trip worthwhile at this time of year.

In taming the western United States, perhaps no factor has been as important as control of water sources. Like the Colorado River, into which it flows, the powerful Gunnison River in central-western Colorado now serves twentieth-century human needs for electricity, water storage, and irrigation. Where once a rushing river eroded ancient rock, the six-mile Gunnison Diversion Tunnel and three dams now control the flow of the Gunnison. These engineering feats have changed the landscape, creating a trio of deep blue lakes, surrounded by the West Elk Mountains to the north and the San Juans to the south.

Curecanti's three lakes—Blue Mesa, Morrow Point, and Crystal—now cover much of the two-billion-year-old rock carved by the river. But nature still dominates these 7,000- to 8,000-foot elevations. Temperatures are cool in summer, frigid in winter, and the land is rugged. Evidence of volcanic activity, such as the spires of Curecanti Needle and the Dillon Pinnacles, is seen throughout the area.

This high country is home to a diverse animal and plant population. Blue herons, bald eagles, ducks, geese, grebes, and other shorebirds frequent the lakeshores, and kokanee salmon and rainbow, brown, brook, and Mackinaw trout thrive below. Prairie dog "towns" still flourish in the surrounding sagebrush, and ground squirrels, rabbits, chipmunks, marmots, and other rodents there provide food for coyotes, golden eagles, and hawks. Rarely observed are black bear, bighorn sheep, and mountain lions.

Morrow Point Lake.

Rangers at Elk Creek Visitor Center will help plan your trip and offer information on the tours, facilities, and interpretive programs available. Of interest are the Gunnison Diversion Tunnel and tours of the Morrow Point Dam powerplant and the narrow-gauge Denver and Rio Grande Railroad exhibit at Cimarron, which commemorates the railroad link forged in 1882 between Salida and Montrose that helped open the West. The railroad supported mining and spurred development of the region between 1882 and 1949.

For travelers crossing the continent on busy Interstate 40 near Grants, New Mexico, the sudden appearance of lava flows alongside the highway is a surprise amid the subtle-hued, mesa-dotted plains. A jagged volcanic landscape assaults the vision. What you are seeing at roadside is the McCarty Flow, the youngest of five major lava flows that have covered this mesa-encircled valley in northwestern New Mexico within the past million years. In fact, the formation of McCarty Flow may have been witnessed by Indians who lived here a thousand years ago.

El Malpais National Monument and the El Malpais National Conservation Area were designated in 1987 to protect these 376,000 acres of spectacular landscape, under an innovative administration by the National Park Service and the Bureau of Land Management. Within this quiet, eerie landscape lie geologic riches, with thirty volcanoes and eighty vents and spatter cones in the area. Geologic activity began at this southern tip of the Colorado Plateau 2 to 4 million years ago with the creation of towering Mount Taylor, an 11,300-foot composite volcano. Erosion then carved the mesas and valley visible today. About a million years ago, a second phase of volcanism began, which resulted in the volcanic features seen at El Malpais (Spanish for "the badland").

Along with the eruption of molten lava and explosive gases came a host of related pyroclastic forms that characterize this landscape. Cinders, ash, bombs, and blocks were spewed out at varying distances from the eruption. In the conservation area, west of the monument, a procession of cinder cones forms the Chain of Craters; Bandera Crater in the national monument is also a cinder cone. Bandera contains famous Candeleria Ice Cave, frozen year-round under a lava mantle in the stable subterranean temperatures of these 6,200- to 8,900-foot elevations. Circular rock structures found near many ice caves here may be linked to Indian use of the caves. El Malpais contains one of the longest lava tube systems in North America. Lava tubes are caused when the surface cools faster than the hotter, faster-flowing, viscous core.

El Malpais is by no means an uninhabited land. Flora and fauna are abundant here. Depending on where you are standing, you may see mountain bluebirds, red-tailed hawks, prairie falcons, American kestrels, killdeer, or others of the 190 bird species recorded here. Rabbits, deer, and mountain lions are among the residents in the varying lava bed, riparian, scrubland, and cliff environments. Specialized life forms, such as blind insects, have been found in the pitch-black underground microenvironments of lava tubes, as well

McCarty Flow and sandstone bluffs.

as on *kupukas* (Hawaiian for "islands"), which are isolated "parks" surrounded by lava. Biologists believe that many kupukas continue to foster undisturbed ecosystems and may eventually yield important information about the natural world.

Human occupation of the area spans 12,000 years. Paleo-Indians once hunted here, followed by Anasazi hunter-gatherers, who settled and farmed the area for more than 500 years, trading with other southwestern cultures. Their modern decendants, the Zuni and Acoma Pueblo Indians, still use this monument for traditional gathering and ceremonial purposes and tell stories of "rivers of fire" that ravaged their homeland. Navajo and Gila Apache Indians, along with Spanish, Mexican, and finally American colonists have all made their mark here. Since the late 1800s, ranching has been a way of life. The nearby town of Grants grew from being a railroad stop to uranium boomtown and now accommodates the new center for El Malpais National Monument administration. A temporary visitor center in downtown Grants provides information and suggestions on drives and hikes in this splendid natural environment.

VISITOR INFORMATION

Just over 178 sq. mi. comprising national monument administered by National Park Service, and 409.4 sq. mi. comprising conservation area administered by Bureau of Land Management. Open year-round, spring through fall usually best times. El Malpais covers a large wilderness area; stop at the information center in Grants, open 8:30 A.M. to 4:30 P.M., to pick up interpretive materials and receive directions about the scenic drive and hiking in the monument/conservation area. Full services available in Grants, at the entrance to the monument; none in the monument or conservation area. Take adequate food and water into El Malpais. For more information, write: Super-intendent, National Park Service, El Malpais National Monument, P.O. Box 939, Grants, NM 87020; or telephone (505) 285-4641. Bureau of Land Management, El Malpais National Conser-vation Area, P.O. Box 846, Grants, NM 87020; telephone (505) 287-7911. www.nps.gov/elma

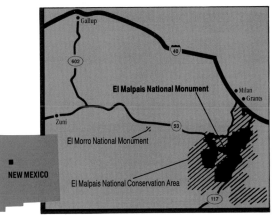

EL MORRO
NATIONAL MONUMENT

Inscription Rock.

VISITOR INFORMATION

Approximately 2 sq. mi. Entrance fee. Open 9 A.M. to 5 P.M. (to 7 P.M. Memorial Day through Labor Day). Visitor center: audiovisual program, museum exhibits, information, bookstore. Half-mile, self-guiding trail around base of Inscription Rock continues to pueblo ruins on top (approximately 2 miles). 9 campsites. Picnicking. For more information, write: Superintendent, El Morro National Monument, Route 2, Box 43, Ramah, NM 87321-8603; or telephone (505) 783-4226. www.nps.gov/elmo

*Spanish inscription,
ca. 1709.*

For at least 700 years, travelers on the high plains of northwestern New Mexico were drawn to a sandstone monolith called El Morro to drink from a permanent pool of water at the rock's base. What draws visitors here today, however, are the inscriptions in the soft stone carved by Anasazi Indians, Spanish explorers, Hispanic settlers, and American emigrants, representing a unique record of the Southwest's checkered history.

El Morro stands in an area of great natural beauty, sure to have impressed even weary travelers of the past. Inspection of the 200-foot-high bluff reveals its origins as the eroded remnant of ancient sand dunes and sediments deposited by a shallow sea millions of years ago. This quiet, mesa-dotted landscape is now clad in a blend of grassland and sagebrush, broken by stands of pinyon, juniper, and stunted Gambel oak mingling with high country ponderosa pine. The skies seem unpopulated and vast, but in summer they become the province of swifts, swallows, and the occasional golden eagle.

For centuries, hunter-gatherers and early farmers used the snowmelt and summer rains that collected in the cracks and the deep pool at the base of El Morro. Then, around 1275, groups of Anasazi coalesced and built two fortified, multi-story pueblos atop either side of El Morro's central box canyon. At this extreme, 7,200-foot elevation, they relied on dry farming, hunting, gathering, and trading. Around 1350, they abandoned their pueblos for reasons still unclear, perhaps going on to join the Zuni people to the west, who today claim the Anasazi as ancestors. A fascinating trail traverses the bluff and passes the excavated larger

ruin of A'ts'ina, which, with its square and round kivas, may reflect Mogollon and Anasazi influences at this cultural crossroads.

Perhaps inspired by Anasazi petroglyphs, Spaniards began to leave their marks on the rock. The first of these was one of the famous names of Southwestern history: Don Juan de Oñate, who established the first Spanish colony in New Mexico. He left his mark on the bluff in 1605, sixty-five years after Coronado's expedition first saw these parts. In 1692, Diego de Vargas autographed the rock as he retook New Mexico for Spain following the 1680 Pueblo Revolt. Throughout these Spanish inscriptions echoes the phrase *pasó por aqui*— "passed by here"—apparently a favorite expression of the time.

The Mexican era of 1821 to 1848 did not make its mark on El Morro, but the arrival of a new wave of English-speaking emigrants is evident from 1849 onwards, following the United States' acquisition of New Mexico. On September 17, 1849, cartographer Lieutenant J. H. Simpson and artist R. H. Kern, assigned to chart the new territory, became the first Americans to document El Morro's many inscriptions.

In 1857 a very different U.S. Army contingent passed through, led by Lieutenant Edward Beale. He attempted to cross the Southwest using camels as pack animals to beat desert conditions. The experiment was cut short by the Civil War and never resurrected, but several beautifully carved inscriptions commemorate the scheme. In July 1858, following the dry, dangerous southern route of the Santa Fe Trail from Missouri, a wagon train of California-bound emigrants came to owe their lives to El Morro's water source. The trip went well until the group was attacked by Mohave Indians along the Colorado River. The survivors returned to Albuquerque by way of El Morro and, undaunted, succeeded in reaching California the next year.

In 1868, the Union Pacific Railroad surveyed the old Zuni-Acoma Trail, on which El Morro sits, for a new railroad. This important event is commemorated by the many inscriptions on the bluff ending with "U.P.R." When the Santa Fe Railroad built a rival line eleven miles to the north, the landmark's long use as a watering hole effectively ended. In 1906, this lonely bluff was designated a national monument, and further carvings on the rock were prohibited. Today, the saga of the Southwest remains written in the rocks of El Morro.

The names of Cochise and Geronimo stand out in any history of the West. During the Indian wars of the late 1800s, these brave Apache leaders and their followers may have fought longer and harder than any other native people to hold onto their homelands. The fierce courage of the Apaches was matched by that of the many American soldiers who fought in unfamiliar desert country to subdue Indian resistance to American westward expansion. Fort Bowie National Historic Site, located in 5,000-foot Apache Pass between southeastern Arizona's Chiricahua and Dos Cabezas mountains, preserves the remains of two successive forts used during the Apache campaign. An old Butterfield Stage Station near Apache Spring is another attraction.

The Chiricahua Apaches were nomadic hunter-gatherers who often raided for food. Ambushes at Apache Pass were so frequent that Spanish travelers called it *Puerto del Dado*, or Pass of Chance. Undoubtedly, these dangers were known to American explorers of the mid-1800s. Even so, the dream of American Manifest Destiny uniting East and West was powerful, and the 1854 Gadsden Purchase of land from Mexico brought the United States closer to unification. In 1858, continental communications improved when John Butterfield started his overland mail link between Missouri and California and built a watering station at Apache Pass.

In the beginning, travelers and mail stages moved through the area largely unhindered, and operators of the way station were on friendly terms with the Apaches. Then, in 1861, an unfortunate event known as the Bascom Affair renewed hostilities. A group of Apaches apparently raided a local ranch, stole livestock, and kidnapped a member of the family. The rancher, convinced that Cochise was responsible, demanded that military authorities bring him to justice. By judicious tactical maneuvering, Second Lieutenant George Bascom found himself face to face with the Apache leader, whom he accused of committing the crime. The furious Cochise immediately fled Bascom's camp, but some of his companions were captured and hanged.

Bloody warfare erupted locally between Apaches and whites and worsened with the advent of the Civil War. Many Southwestern forts were abandoned as Americans chose sides in the conflict. Western territory now lay unprotected from Confederate armies intent on reaching California goldfields and claiming the Arizona Territory for the Confederacy. In 1862, to help counter the expected Confederate invasion of New Mexico and to avoid ambushes of military supplies, Union volunteers, led by Brigadier General James H. Carleton, built the first Fort Bowie, in Apache

Garrison flag and remains of guardhouse.

Pass. Soldiers toughed out rudimentary conditions and resisted Indian incursions here until they were relieved by regular troops at the end of the Civil War in 1866. A second, better-situated Fort Bowie was started in 1868, which eventually included barracks, officers' quarters, storehouses, a trader's store, and a hospital, all built of adobe.

In 1871, a peace treaty was negotiated with Cochise that gave the Chiricahua Apaches a 3,000-square-mile reservation. However, most Apaches found an agricultural reservation life intolerable, and tensions mounted, exacerbated by Cochise's natural death in 1874. Hoping to avoid revolt, the government moved the Apaches to another reservation, but renegades, led by Apache warrior Geronimo, managed to escape to Mexico's Sierra Madre, where they attacked settlers along the border. Twice Geronimo was recaptured, only to escape again.

In 1886, General Nelson A. Miles succeeded in subduing Geronimo. The Apaches were sent to forts in Florida and Alabama and eventually resettled at Fort Sill, Oklahoma, where Geronimo died in 1909. Fort Bowie, having fulfilled its mission, was officially abandoned in 1894. Today, visitors reach the fort and the mail station by walking the 1.5-mile trail to the weathered ruins, which stand like ghostly sentinels guarding the memory of a turbulent past.

VISITOR INFORMATION

1.5 sq. mi. Park open year-round. Visitor center open 8 A.M. to 5 P.M.: exhibits, information, bookstore. Ranger talks by advance reservation only. 1.5-mile trail leads to ruins from graded Apache Pass Road, interpretive signs along the way. Bad weather may make road impassable; call for information. When hiking, wear clothing appropriate for desert extremes. No camping or picnicking at site. Nearest services, including lodging and campgrounds, are in Bowie or Willcox. Chiricahua National Monument, twenty-five miles away, has National Park Service campground; several campgrounds in Coronado National Forest south of monument. For more information, write: Park Ranger, Fort Bowie National Historic Site, P.O. Box 158, Bowie, AZ 85605; or telephone (520) 847-2500. www.nps.gov/fobo

FORT DAVIS
NATIONAL HISTORIC SITE

Officers' Row.

VISITOR INFORMATION

460 acres. Entrance fee. Open year-round, except Christmas Day. Hours are 8 A.M. to 5 P.M. (to 6 P.M., Memorial Day through Labor Day). Visitor center: audiovisual program, exhibits, information, bookstore. Audio presentation of 1875 Dress Retreat Parade daily. Self-guiding tour of grounds and several buildings. Tours and demonstrations conducted by costumed interpreters in summer. Hiking along nature trails and in Davis Mountains State Park. Weather at this 4,900-foot elevation is hot and occasionally wet in summer, cool and windy in winter and spring. No camping at fort, but picnicking allowed. Nearest campground and lodging is in adjoining Davis Mountains State Park. For more information, write: Superintendent, Fort Davis National Historic Site, P.O. Box 1456, Fort Davis, TX 79734; or telephone (915) 426-3224. www.nps.gov/foda

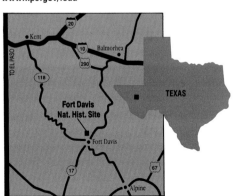

Following American acquisition of vast new lands from Mexico in 1848, settlement of the West was a foregone conclusion. A trickle of immigrants became a flood in 1849, after the discovery of gold in California. Many attempted to avoid the snowy mountains of central and northern cross-country routes by taking the southern branch of the San Antonio–El Paso Road across the desert plains. Here, aside from heat and thirst, the greatest danger was attack by Apache or Comanche Indians.

In 1854, as Indian incursions worsened, the army decided to build a fort beside the Apache (later Davis) Mountains to protect precious water sources and to safeguard travelers crossing West Texas. It was named Fort Davis after Secretary of War Jefferson Davis, who would shortly become president of the Confederacy.

American expansionism, Civil War, the abolition of slavery, and long-running Indian wars all affected Fort Davis during its thirty-seven years of service. The fifty original pine-slab-and-stone structures, built and occupied by six companies of the Eighth U.S. Infantry, were scattered throughout a box canyon near Limpia Creek. From here, soldiers struggled against Indian attacks and provided escort for government supply wagons, early overland mail lines, and immigrants.

At the start of the Civil War in 1861, Confederates took over Fort Davis and briefly enjoyed friendly relations with the Apaches, which ended when Apache raiders stole some of their livestock. A party of soldiers led by Lieutenant Rueben Mays was subsequently massacred while pursuing the raiders, forcing the Confederates to fight Indians as well as Union troops. In 1862, when the Confederates failed to take New Mexico, Fort Davis was again abandoned and only reoccupied when victorious Federal soldiers returned to rebuild the wrecked fort in 1867.

More than sixty large stone and adobe structures gradually were built on the plain. Fort Davis became one of the largest military installations in the Southwest, with barracks, officers' quarters, kitchens, a military hospital, a chapel, and a headquarters building. Echoing the changing times, Fort Davis and other Texas forts were manned by newly freed black slaves commanded by white officers. The bravery of the black troops during the ensuing Indian Wars led their enemies to call them "buffalo soldiers." The buffalo soldiers were particularly successful in Texas and Arizona in fighting bands of renegade Apaches led by chiefs such as Victorio and Geronimo, resulting in peace treaties with the Indians in 1886.

Soldiers continued to drill and patrol the Chihuahuan Desert for another five years, but Fort Davis had now outlived its usefulness. The fort was abandoned in 1891, but its importance in Southwestern history was officially recognized when it was designated a national historic site in 1961. Approximately twenty-five buildings have now been restored, and the remains of others still stand. Visitors to Fort Davis today may tour what is now considered the best-preserved frontier fort in the Southwest and vividly experience what life was like here during the late 1800s.

Enlisted men's equipment.

FORT UNION
NATIONAL MONUMENT

For dusty travelers on the 800-mile-long Santa Fe Trail linking Missouri and New Mexico, the Fort Union compound on the western edge of a windswept valley near the plains in northeastern New Mexico must have been a heavenly sight after many tiring, anxious weeks on the trail.

The Santa Fe Trail opened in 1821, after Mexico won its independence from Spain. Thirty years later, Fort Union was built strategically close to the junction of two branches of the trail. Now, for the first time, troops were garrisoned close enough to the scene of Indian hostilities to be able to react to them. With army assistance, westward expansion, trade, and communication began to boom.

For another thirty years, traders, supply wagons, mail stages, and the occasional settler sought safe passage through the area. Over time, many others learned to call the remote outpost home. As Fort Union grew from a small log fort to an imposing landmark massed against the Sangre de Cristo Mountains, so too did the permanent population. By the 1870s, officers, enlisted men, families, and civilian workers were living at the fort, then one of the largest in the Southwest. Today, the only evidence of this time are the ruins of the final fort, the faint outlines of two earlier forts, and the deep wagon ruts of the Santa Fe Trail close to the monument.

The first Fort Union was built by Colonel Edwin Sumner and his men in 1851. Following the 1846–1848 Mexican-American War that won New Mexico for the United States, Sumner was charged with protecting new United States citizens—both Hispanic and Anglo—from attacks by Native Americans. One of his first acts was to abandon army headquarters in Santa Fe, then a rowdy town he described as a "sink of vice and extravagance," and to move closer to areas frequented by Jicarilla Apaches, Kiowas, Utes, and Comanches. Remembering the strategic location of this valley in northeastern New Mexico, Sumner had his men build a small, log-and-earth garrison here. For ten years, the soldiers at this first fort braved rotting, bug-ridden quarters, ran a supply depot, and scrapped with neighboring Indian tribes who increasingly saw their vital resources slipping away to whites.

During the Civil War, many of Fort Union's officers left to join the Confederacy, and a major confrontation with the Texas Confederates for control of Fort Union and Colorado brewed. A new commander, Colonel Canby, supplemented the few remaining soldiers at Fort Union with a battalion of Colorado Volunteers. Under Canby's orders, a star-shaped, semisubterranean, earthworks fort was constructed, and Fort Union prepared for

Historic commercial wagon in Mechanics Corral.

battle. But the Star Fort never saw action. During the Battle of Glorieta Pass, fought east of the Rio Grande, the Colorado Volunteers, along with regular troops and New Mexico Volunteer units, accidentally stumbled upon and destroyed all the supply wagons of the advancing Confederates. Unable to support a further offensive, the Confederates retreated, and New Mexico was saved for the Union.

The final fort, whose remains you see today, was built between 1863 and 1869 to serve as a central supply post for the Western armed forces and as a base of operations against Indian incursions that continued until 1875. The new fort cost one million dollars and was built of limewashed adobe, with porticoed homes for the officers. It had a military post, a large quartermaster's depot and warehouses, the largest hospital in the area, a jail, corrals, workshops, offices, quarters, a parade ground, and a sutler store. The site of the original log fort was reused as an arsenal.

By 1879, however, the railroad extended to nearby Las Vegas, New Mexico, beginning the decline of the fort, which was finally abandoned in 1891. The site became a national monument in 1956, and the Santa Fe Trail was designated a national scenic trail in 1987. The men and women whose lives crossed at Fort Union are not forgotten.

VISITOR INFORMATION

720 acres. Entrance fee. 8 A.M. to 6 P.M. (summer). Spring, summer, and fall best times. Visitor center: audiovisual program, museum exhibits, bookstore, information. Summer "living history" interpretive programs. Self-guiding trail with pushbutton audio vignettes. Picnicking, but no camping at monument; nearest campground at Storrie Lake State Park, 5 miles northwest of Las Vegas. Food and lodging in Las Vegas, 28 miles south. No public transportation to monument. For more information, write: Superintendent, Fort Union National Monument, P.O. Box 127, Watrous, NM 87753; or telephone (505) 425-8025. www.nps.gov/foun

GILA CLIFF DWELLINGS NATIONAL MONUMENT

View of Cliff Dweller Canyon from Cave Five.

VISITOR INFORMATION

533 acres. Visitor center operated jointly by National Park Service and U.S. Forest Service; open 8 A.M. to 5 P.M. (summer), 8 A.M. to 4:30 P.M. (winter): audiovisual program, exhibits, information, bookstore. All facilities closed December 25 and New Year's Day, except Trail to the Past, which is open 24 hours all year. Gila Cliff Dwellings Contact Station open limited hours: exhibits, some interpretive activities. One-mile self-guided loop trail through cliff dwellings open 8 A.M. to 6 P.M. (summer), 9 A.M. to 4 P.M. (rest of year). Unexcavated TJ Ruin may be entered only by guided tour; advance reservations required. Improved campgrounds and picnic areas available nearby in Gila National Forest. Nearest lodging and supplies in Gila Hot Springs, where horse rentals and guided pack trips into Gila Wilderness are also available. Note: NM Highway 15 to monument from Silver City is narrow and very winding; allow 2 hours. NM Highway 35, which is slightly longer, is recommended for trailers and longer vehicles. For more information, write: Park Ranger, Gila Cliff Dwellings National Monument, Route 11, Box 100, Silver City, NM 88061; or telephone (505) 536-9461. www.nps.gov/gicl

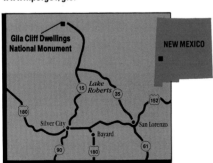

Of the three main cultures that came to dominate the prehistoric Southwest, the Mogollon have traditionally been considered the least complex. Evidence suggests, however, that these people were in fact farming and making pottery earlier than any other Southwestern group. Perhaps it was merely their isolation in New Mexico's rugged Mogollon Mountains that prevented the mobility and exchange of ideas that allowed other cultures to advance. Whatever the reason for their simple lifestyle, the Mogollon began their rapid adoption of greater cultural sophistication only toward the tenth century as contact with Anasazi traders increased and Mogollon farmers adopted and synthesized new Anasazi ways.

The focus at the monument is the sheltered cliff dwellings in the caves above Cliff Dweller Canyon. We can only speculate about what forced the Mogollon there in A.D. 1270. It may have been population growth, raids by other groups, internal fighting, or perhaps depletion of resources following drought. For centuries, though, cliff dwellings were unknown here, although some Mogollon practices, such as the use of great kivas for ceremonies, paralleled pueblo living elsewhere. These canyon dwellers lived in subterranean pit houses, grew typical Southwestern crops by the Gila River, and scouted mountain slopes for additional foods. They hunted deer, rabbits, and other small animals through cool forests of Douglas fir and ponderosa and pinyon pine, which provided timber for mud-and-wood roofs. Nuts and berries were gathered for food, and yuccas were used for clothing, edible fruits, and medicine. Mogollon artisans fashioned rough russet-colored pots with a stable round base for cooking and storage, which they gradually improved in shape and decorated with simple red designs. The Mogollon also excelled at making necklaces

from turquoise stones, which would eventually be traded for copper bells from Mexico, shells, and other goods.

The Mogollon admitted Anasazi refugees in A.D. 1000 and soon learned to build rectangular, Anasazi-style villages, or pueblos. Mogollon people living near the Mimbres River developed superb pottery that featured animals, humans, and mythological creatures painted in black on a white background. Mimbres pottery remains highly prized today. After a few Mogollon moved to the cliffs in 1270, their culture continued to thrive for a short time, then quickly came to an end, perhaps being completely absorbed by the Anasazi who moved on in search of better farmlands. The forty apartment-style rooms built high in the cliffs were empty by the early 1300s.

Nomadic Apaches moved into the Gila Wilderness, fighting anyone encroaching on their land. Spanish, Mexican, and eventually American settlers were systematically repelled until determined U.S. government forces in 1885 forced the Apache out of their homelands. The Chiricahua Apaches, whose territory included the Mogollon Mountains, were subdued, rounded up, and sent to Florida for incarceration, ending another era of Native American dominance in the Gila.

Gila Cliff Dwellings is located alongside the nation's first designated wilderness area, which was established in 1924. The monument itself was set aside to protect the cliff dwellings in 1907 and expanded to include another prehistoric site in 1962. Since 1975, the U.S. Forest Service and the National Park Service have run the monument jointly, with the forest service responsible for administration and interpretation on a day-to-day basis. Until recently, this remote monument was hard to reach and little known. Today, a winding, paved road leads to it, leaving the adjoining wilderness pristine.

Padre Bay, Lake Powell.

VISITOR INFORMATION

Approximately 1,961 sq. mi. Open year-round; spring, summer, and fall best times. Carl Hayden Visitor Center open 8 A.M. to 5 P.M. with extended summer hours: exhibits, interpretive presentations, bookstore. Self-guided tours of Glen Canyon Dam and Powerplant year-round with additional guided tours during the summer offered by Glen Canyon Natural History Association in cooperation with Bureau of Reclamation. The Bureau also controls water releases from Lake Powell. Free multi-image slide programs on the dam and park are offered by the National Park Service. Concessions provide equipment rentals, marinas, lodging, food, and other services. 5 marinas. 4 public campgrounds. Many undeveloped campsites on shores of Lake Powell. Camping on southern lake shore by permission of the Navajo Nation only. Powell Museum and full services can be found in Page. For more information, write: Superintendent, Glen Canyon National Recreation Area, P.O. Box 1507, Page, AZ 86040; or telephone (520) 608-6404. U.S. Bureau of Reclamation, Office of Public Affairs, P.O. Box 11568, Salt Lake City, UT 84147. www.nps.gov/glca

Glen Canyon National Recreation Area, which sits on the Arizona-Utah border, is a magnet for visitors to the desert Southwest. Here is a heady mixture of fantastic, sheer-walled rock canyons, deep blue skies reflected in shimmering waters, and seemingly endless opportunities for land and water activities.

The dominant feature of the recreation area is Lake Powell, formed in 1963 when Glen Canyon Dam was completed. The dam was authorized by the 1956 Colorado River Storage Project Act. Following seven years of construction, during which time Glen Canyon Bridge was built and the new town of Page grew up, Glen Canyon Dam began operation. The dam was built for water storage, flood control, irrigation, generation of hydroelectric power, and river regulation.

Lake Powell, the second largest manmade lake in the Western Hemisphere, extends 186 miles upstream from the dam; at full capacity the reservoir holds 27 million acre-feet of water, has a surface area of 255 square miles, and 1,960 miles of shoreline. But the wonderland that attracts so many modern-day visitors has a hidden story to tell, for before Glen Canyon was flooded, it was the

(continued)

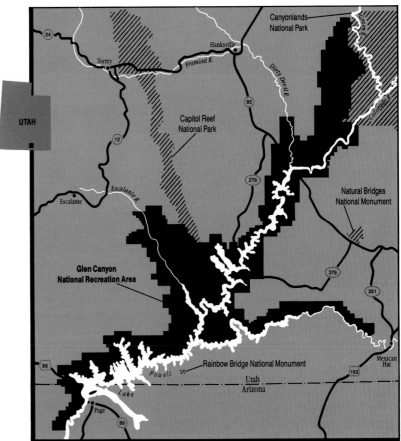

Plains prickly pear cactus.

haunt of many plants and animals and native people, who made their homes beneath the sheltering canyon walls.

Water activities, such as boating, water-skiing, wind surfing, and swimming predominate on Lake Powell, well served by five marinas. But there is much more to see and do at Glen Canyon. Here, marine and dune sediments gave rise to spectacular sandstone and shale formations carved by wind and water, and natural bridges formed in side canyons such as Escalante Canyon and at Rainbow Bridge National Monument (discussed separately in this book). The bridges were carved by streams that, over the millennia, incised deep, meandering canyons. Seasonal flooding turned these streams into torrents, causing them to break through their rocky meanders to forge a more direct path through the canyon. Islandlike buttes are further evidence of erosion.

In Escalante Canyon, evidence of Archaic hunter-gatherer, Anasazi, and Fremont Indian use has been found. In Escalante and elsewhere in the Glen Canyon region both Fremont and Anasazi people left behind rock art that eloquently reflects their differing world views. As drought and other pressures forced these groups away from the canyons, newly arriving Navajos, Utes, and Paiutes wandered through in search of game and wild food plants. The Navajo Reservation abuts Glen Canyon on the south and has provided sanctuary since the tribe's arrival here, probably around A.D. 1300. As Spanish exploration, then American settlement, of the region grew in the eighteenth and nineteenth centuries, Navajos fought to keep their land, stealing from pueblos and Mormon homesteads to reestablish dominion. In 1864, the Navajos were forced by the U.S. Army to relocate to Fort Sumner, New Mexico, in a reservation experiment that failed

Gunsight Butte, Navajo Mountain in distance, Lake Powell.

Anasazi petroglyphs, Defiance House.

As clouds scud across the sky, rock shapes and hues change in a never-ending shadow play, inviting boaters on Lake Powell to contemplate the natural beauty of the surrounding landscape. Although this desert is cooler than many, temperature extremes still relegate most animal activity to nighttime, when alert hunters like the coyote and gray fox pursue their prey of jackrabbits and kangaroo rats. Reptiles like collared lizards and Western rattlesnakes sleepily endure daytime conditions, in contrast with the white antelope squirrel which relishes the daylight hours. Expect to see (or hear) canyon wrens, horned larks, sage sparrows, and raptors like red-tailed hawks and peregrine falcons. Willows, tamarisk, cottonwoods, and various sedges and grasses grow in watered side canyons, while gardens of smaller moisture-loving plants, such as maidenhair ferns, thrive in shady seeps. At higher elevations, pinyon-juniper forest grips sandy soil, its scrubby appearance relieved in spring by colorful wildflowers.

miserably. The Navajos returned here to graze sheep, farm, and weave rugs in 1868. Mormon missionary Jacob Hamblin became friendly with Hopis and Paiutes, fostering Anglo-Indian harmony and a number of conversions in the late nineteenth century. By 1880, these ardent home-steaders were joined by ranchers whose cattle, over a ten-year period, overgrazed the land so badly that it has never recovered.

Glen Canyon's labyrinthian country often sheltered fugitives as well as pioneers. The celebrated Butch Cassidy and his Wild Bunch holed up at Robbers Roost, just outside park limits, and rustled range cattle as well as robbed banks and transcontinental trains. Until today, this rugged environment has attracted only the fearless and adventurous—on both sides of the law—and it still commands our respect today.

Sunset from Yaki Point.

The region . . . is, of course, altogether valueless. It can be approached only from the south, and after entering it there is nothing to do but leave. Ours has been the first, and will doubtless be the last, party of whites to visit this profitless locality. It seems intended that the Colorado River, along the greater portion of its lonely and majestic way, shall be forever unvisited and undisturbed.

In 1858, federal government surveyor Lieutenant Joseph Ives offered these immortal words in his report on the Grand Canyon region of the lower Colorado River in Arizona, which lay within one of America's newest territories. How wrong he was! Nearly four million people a year now peer into this mile-deep gash in the earth, searching for the ribbon of water that cut this fantastic rockscape. These days, the Grand Canyon is on the itinerary of almost every traveler to the western United States.

Hiking trails, mule rides, river rafting trips, campgrounds, hotels, shuttle buses, cars, and all-weather roads make visiting the Grand Canyon in the late twentieth century relatively easy, but it wasn't always so. For centuries, the canyon was more barrier than attraction—an area intermittently used by hunter-gatherer Indians and for a time by the Anasazi. But eyewitness accounts by Spanish conquistadors in the 1500s and American prospectors in the early 1800s slowly piqued interest in the canyon's inner secrets back east.

Starting with Ives's exploration of the lower Colorado River, and reaching a zenith with surveyor John Wesley Powell's adventuresome river runs in 1869 and 1871–1872, a procession of scientists, prospectors, homesteaders, and early concessionaires blazed trails through this wild country. Spurred by growing public enthusiasm and the backing of President Theodore Roosevelt in 1906, the Grand Canyon became in quick succession a game reserve, a national forest, a national monument (in 1908), and finally (in 1919), a national park. Since 1975, the national park has also encompassed the western portion of the Grand Canyon, a remote volcanic area known as the Tuweep Unit, which for many years was preserved as Grand Canyon National Monument.

A mere six million years of erosion by the Colorado River, along with rain, flooding, and wind, have created this 277-mile-long, 18-mile-wide crevice in our planet's surface. Tantalizing glimpses of half of the earth's five billion years of history are revealed here. From canyon bottom to rim, the drama of four geologic eras is exposed in succeeding rock strata. Evidence of ancient mountains, several seas, rivers, deserts, volcanoes, and the creatures that inhabited them is visible in the rocks. As you descend into the canyon, you will see marine fossils entombed in the pale Kaibab Limestone of the rims; farther down are the looping strata of petrified sand dunes formed during a period of desertification; and at canyon bottom is

(continued)

VISITOR INFORMATION

1,904 sq. mi. Spring and fall best times.

SOUTH RIM: Visitor center open year-round, 8 A.M. to 5 P.M. (with extended hours in summer): audiovisual and interpretive programs, bookstore; Tusayan and Yavapai museums. 9 rim-to-river hikes of varying difficulty (bring plenty of water), rim drive. Hiking overnight into backcountry by permit only, obtainable by mail from Backcountry Reservations Office (BRO), P.O. Box 129, Grand Canyon, AZ 86023; or tel. (520) 638-7888 for further information. Note: Reserve early as popular trails can fill up a year in advance; however, the BRO maintains a waiting list for permits that become available through cancellations. Rafting and mule rides offered through concessionaires; the National Park Service will provide a list on request. Complete visitor facilities available. Reserve well ahead for El Tovar Hotel and Bright Angel Lodge (bookable 23 months in advance), Phantom Ranch at canyon bottom (bookable 11 months in advance), and 4 other motels. Tel: (303) 297-2757, fax: (303) 297-3175. 50 campsites in Desert View Campground (first-come, first-served) and 320 campsites in Mather Campground (by reservation). For campground reservations call 1-800-365-CAMP. Commercial and Forest Service campgrounds nearby. Accommodation also available at Tusayan, just outside the park entrance.

(continued)

NORTH RIM: Open May through October; National Park Service visitor information available in lobby of Grand Canyon Lodge; interpretive programs, bookstore. 4 rim-to-river hikes of varying difficulty (bring plenty of water), rim drive. Mule rides, bus tours, and river tours through concessionaires. Limited visitor facilities available. Reserve well ahead for Grand Canyon Lodge (bookable 23 months in advance), tel. (303) 297-2757. There are 2 motels north of park. 82 National Park Service campsites. Call 1-800-365-CAMP for reservations. 125 sites in commercial and forest service camp-grounds nearby. Open camping in surrounding Kaibab National Forest. For more information, write: Superintendent, Grand Canyon National Park, P.O. Box 129, Grand Canyon, AZ 86023; or telephone (520) 638-7888. www.nps.gov/grca

the dark Vishnu Schist that made up Precambrian mountains two billion years ago. Nowhere else in the world is such a clear geological time line so readily apparent.

Following successive volcanism, erosion, and sedimentation, this region was compressed and uplifted beginning about 65 million years ago to form the Colorado Plateau, of which the Grand Canyon is part. Continued uplift and tilting occurred and spawned the Colorado River, which proceeded to change this landscape forever. The debris-laden river cut down into underlying rock, sculpting the Grand Canyon. Side streams, wind, and extreme temperatures then widened the main canyon and also created the many side canyons and other eroded forms in the Grand Canyon. The eroded material has been carried away by the river to its final destination, the Gulf of California. Conical buttes, known as "temples," dominate the canyon skyline. In 1880, geologist Clarence Dutton, a student of Eastern religion, named Vishnu and Shiva temples, as well as many other formations here.

Elevations from 1,300 feet at canyon bottom rising to 8,200 feet at the North Rim have created four life zones within the park's bounds—Lower and Upper Sonoran Desert, Transition, and Canadian. Consequently, one of the joys of a descent into the Grand Canyon is the chance to encounter a wide diversity of plants and wildlife. At the more accessible South Rim, pinyon-juniper forests and ponderosa pines intersperse with hardy cliff rose and sagebrush. This plant community supports many Upper Sonoran and Transition zone inhabitants, such as chipmunks, squirrels, coyotes, cottontails, porcupines, and mule deer. Lugubrious ravens hover overhead, sharing the airways with Steller's jays, woodpeckers, and great horned owls.

The higher, cooler North Rim enjoys additional moisture, allowing stands of fir, spruce, aspen, and ponderosa pine to flourish, surrounded by lush meadows sporting carpets of brilliant sunflowers, goldenrod, and asters in summertime. Pocket gophers and other rodents provide food for coyotes and bobcats, while mountain lions feed on mule deer. In the canyon bottom, a most startling contrast exists where dry desert abuts riparian habitat. On the ledges, shy bighorn sheep inspect cracks in the rock for forage, picking among cacti and yucca and startling chuckwallas, collared lizards, and the occasional rattlesnake. Mingling with the sound of water trickling over river boulders and the exuberant shouts of river runners is the sweet song of the canyon wren, which shares the streamside environment with ducks, great blue herons, and even sandpipers. The canyon is home to butterflies, too, with the Western tiger swallowtail preferring the rim and the monarch flitting above river shallows. The river jumps with rainbow trout and carp—cold-water fish that have replaced native chub and squawfish in the colder waters that now emerge from Lake Powell.

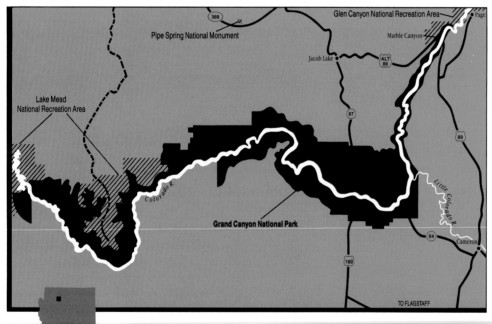

Colorado River seen from Toroweep.

Pinyon pines along the South Bass Trail.

Hiking in the canyon is like climbing a mountain in reverse—the return journey is tougher than the descent. Popular hikes here are the 9.5-mile Bright Angel Trail, which descends from the South Rim, crossing the canyon bottom to historic Phantom Ranch and the Bright Angel Campground. From the North Rim, the 14.2-mile North Kaibab Trail provides a good introduction to that side of the canyon. Other trails of varying difficulty are available, though not maintained. River rafting trips, lasting five days to three weeks, draw thousands each year and provide a memorable experience of the Grand Canyon. But for more sedate visitors, there are also beautiful rim drives offering many canyon overlooks. Sunrise and sunset are particularly stunning from Bright Angel Point on the North Rim and from Desert View on the South Rim. The Watchtower at Desert View, designed in 1932 by Mary Jane Colter, provides the highest point from which to view the Colorado River and the Painted Desert. Tusayan Museum, just to the west, interprets adjoining Tusayan Ruin, the twelfth-century remains of an Anasazi Indian village.

Of interest, too, are the rustic Grand Canyon Lodge on the North Rim, designed by architect Gilbert Stanley Underwood in 1928, and El Tovar Hotel, built on the South Rim in 1905 and considered one of the first examples of "rustic architecture." Rail travel to the canyon has become fashionable once again with the reopening of the Grand Canyon Railway, which brings visitors from Williams, Arizona. Another popular attraction is the Kolb Photographic Studio. This historic studio belonged to the adventurous Kolb brothers, the first people to film a Grand Canyon river run.

Wotans Throne and Vishnu Temple seen from Mather Point.

Claret cup cactus.

Greenland Lake, North Rim.

Blue columbine.

The Watchtower, Desert View.

12th century Anasazi pottery.

GREAT SAND DUNES
NATIONAL MONUMENT

*Sunset on dune
ridge and Sangre de
Cristo Mountains.*

VISITOR INFORMATION

55 sq. mi. Visitor center open daily (except federal holidays in winter) from 8 A.M. to 4:30 P.M., with extended summer hours: information, interpretive programs, exhibits, bookstore. Montville Nature Trail and longer Mosca Pass Trail are recommended. Four-wheel-drive tours operated in summer on Medano Pass Primitive Road by concessionaire. Pinyon Flats Campground operated on first-come, first-served basis. Water available April to October only. No food available in monument; come prepared. Nearest full services are in Alamosa 38 miles south. For more information, write: Superintendent, Great Sand Dunes National Monument, 11999 Highway 150, Mosca, CO 81146; or telephone (719) 378-2312. www.nps.gov/grsa

The tallest sand dunes in North America are not found on any beach—they are at Great Sand Dunes National Monument, nestled in the lap of the Sangre de Cristo Mountains in the San Luis Valley of Colorado.

Unique geographical factors have built these 700-foot dunes. For millennia, the Rio Grande, which bisects the valley, has carried sediments down from the volcanic San Juan Mountains to the west and deposited them on its bed and on its banks. At some point, though, the river changed course in this valley, leaving the sandy deposits victim to the powerful southwesterly winds that sweep through. Sometimes reaching more than forty miles an hour, these winds scoop up the grains of sand and buffet the 14,000-foot Sangre de Cristos. The sand is too heavy to funnel through the mountain passes, and as the winds continue their passage out of the valley, their sandy cargo is left cradled at the base of the foothills.

Many people are surprised that the dunes, which seize the imagination with their ever-changing shapes and colors, don't blow away. Yet, their shifting surfaces are underlaid by cores that are remarkably stable due in large part to their high moisture content, from mountain streams, creeks, and groundwater. After a while, Indian ricegrass, blowout grass, scurfpea, and prairie sunflower insinuate their way onto the vast slopes, stabilizing them further.

Those who come here to hike, camp, four-wheel drive on designated roads, play in the dunes, and observe nature are well rewarded. Half-mile-long Montville Nature Trail is an easy loop from the visitor center, through a section of Mosca Canyon and over Mosca Creek, leading through pinyon-juniper woodland, desert, and riparian habitats. The woodlands shelter deer, coyotes, occasional elk and black bear, and chattery black-billed magpies. Water-loving willows and cottonwoods line the creek and provide a chance for walkers to cool off.

Yucca and prickly pear grow near the base of the hot, dry dunes, and some creatures actually manage to live here. This is the domain of the kangaroo rat, which metabolizes its own water. Three unique insects also make the dunes their home: the Great Sand Dunes tiger beetle, the giant sand treader camel cricket, and a circus beetle.

For an even more fascinating hike, explore 3.5-mile Mosca Pass Trail, which climbs from the nature trail through the Rio Grande National Forest for a wonderful view of the valley and nearby mountains. This trip takes you into cool mountain forests of Douglas fir, aspen, ponderosa pine, and Rocky Mountain maple.

Explorer John C. Fremont may have used Medano Pass on his way through this region in 1848–1849. Four years later, railroad surveyor Captain John Gunnison, for whom Colorado's Gunnison River is named, also explored the area and recommended that a transcontinental railroad traverse these mountains (the railroad was never built). As Americans began to push west in search of gold and new land to settle, some chose to homestead this remote area. One settler, Frank Hastings, operated a toll gate and store on Mosca Pass near fur trapper Antoine Roubidoux's old trading post; Hastings's store later served as post office to Montville's small community and can still be seen on the Mosca Pass Trail. Life was hard here. Homesteaders farmed and ranched, irrigating fruits and vegetables and other crops with canals and runoff. As competition for grazing land grew, range wars broke out in the 1880s, leading to federal establishment of timber reserves. In the teens, these became the first national forests, of which Rio Grande National Forest is one.

Prairie sunflower.

El Capitan.

Agave.

The imposing Guadalupe Mountains act as an enormous step between the broken plains of southern New Mexico and the torrid Chihuahuan Desert extending north into Texas from Mexico. With little fanfare, the desert gives way abruptly to the ramparts of the mountains, where spectacular dropoffs characterize the east, west, and south sides of the fifty-mile-long range. A natural divide is found at Guadalupe Pass between the Guadalupe and Delaware mountains, near the foot of the monolith, El Capitan.

Venture beyond these blank walls, though, and the true glory of the Guadalupes becomes apparent. Clustering around springs in McKittrick and Pine Springs canyons are maples, oaks, and walnut trees, whose autumn foliage is unrivaled in the Southwest. The park, Texas's largest designated wilderness, is mostly backcountry and is best explored on the eighty miles of hiking trails that connect the desert, interior canyons, and high mountain slopes.

These mountains are part of what was once a 400-mile-long reef, which formed along a shelf in a Permian sea about 250 million years ago. The sea was bordered by tidal flats and lagoons and had three large bays, now the Delaware, Midland, and Marfa basins. The reef adjoins the Delaware Basin and is surrounded by the Glass and Apache mountain ranges. It was formed from lime secretions from sponges, calcareous algae, and the surrounding water, which were buried by layers of salt, gypsum, potash, and other sediments when

the sea eventually dried up. During the upheaval that formed the Guadalupes 10 to 12 million years ago, the rock strata entombing the fossil reef were exposed to the weathering forces of wind, water, and ice, allowing the horseshoe-shaped reef to reemerge. The park's Permian Reef Geology Trail offers visitors a chance to examine the reef's features close up.

The principal erosion here occurs when rainwater made acidic by carbon dioxide in the air and organic matter in the soil dissolves limestone along stress fractures. When the solution evaporates, crystalline calcite deposits remain, often forming flowstone, or travertine, a marblelike stone found in caves, seeps, and streambeds in places like McKittrick Canyon. Oil and gas also became trapped in pockets within Permian shales, thereby creating the large Permian Oilfield east of the Guadalupes. Early oil exploration prompted the first studies of the mountains' unique geology. Geologist Wallace Pratt fell in love with the Guadalupes and bought large tracts of land in beautiful McKittrick Canyon, where his cabin may still be seen. It is largely thanks to him and Judge J. C. Hunter, a local rancher, that Guadalupe Mountains National Park was set aside in 1972 to protect the unique geology and wildlife of these mountains.

(continued)

VISITOR INFORMATION

135 sq. mi. Open year-round, weather permitting; visitor center open 8 A.M. to 4:30 P.M., with extended hours in summer. Visitor center at Pine Springs on U.S. 62/180: audiovisual program, exhibits, information, interpretive activities (summer), bookstore; information station at McKittrick Canyon. Hiking is the best way to see the park, but 2 historic areas close to visitor center may be reached by passenger vehicle. 12 trails of varying difficulty and length highlight the geology, history, and natural diversity of park. Temperatures at different park elevations vary widely all year; come prepared and carry a good topographical map and adequate water. Campgrounds at Pine Springs and in Dog Canyon (66 campsites); 10 primitive campsites in backcountry with permit. Picnicking at Pine Springs, Dog Canyon, and McKittrick Canyon. No services in park; nearest gas, food, and RV park 10 miles west of park. More facilities at Whites City, Carlsbad, Van Horn, and El Paso. For more information, write: Superintendent, Guadalupe Mountains National Park, H.C. 60, Box 400, Salt Flat, TX 79847-9400; or telephone (915) 828-3251. www.nps.gov/gumo

*Maple and madrone
trees in McKittrick
Canyon.*

*Entrance to
McKittrick Canyon.*

*Fossil in Capitan
Limestone.*

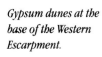

*Gypsum dunes at the
base of the Western
Escarpment.*

Park elevations range from 3,660 feet in the desert to 8,749 feet at the top of Guadalupe Peak, Texas's highest mountain. The desert is home to water-saving plants, such as creosote bush, agave, and cactus, and to creatures like lizards, snakes, and the kangaroo rat, which metabolizes its own water from seeds. Most of these animals are nocturnal, avoiding the harsh daytime temperatures. In the heart of the mountains, clustering around the springs that feed the creeks in McKittrick and Pine Springs canyons, are trees like ponderosa pine and Texas madrone. Springs in these canyons are the result of high-country rainfall that penetrates the limestone and emerges at the base of the cliffs. Tanagers, canyon wrens, and other birds find plenty to eat and drink here, as do deer and coyotes that prowl in the lengthening evening shadows. Emblematic of these cool, damp areas are maidenhair fern, columbines, and other plants that form delightful gardens around the seeps.

Higher up the climate becomes moister and cooler, providing a suitable habitat for Douglas fir, ponderosa, and limber pine in dense, dark stands. These trees are a relict forest isolated on the Guadalupes after the Ice Age, surrounded by the lowlands of the Chihuahuan Desert. The mountains are also a sanctuary for creatures generally found farther north, such as elk and black bear. Birds like nuthatches, mountain chickadees, and migratory warblers thrive here.

Paleo-Indians hunted mammoth in this region 10,000 years ago. Much later, Apaches from the north entered the region. They lived a nomadic hunter-gatherer existence, but also alternately traded with and raided Pueblo Indians along the Rio Grande, a tactic later used on Spanish and Mexican settlers. After the United States acquired vast new Southwestern territory from Mexico in 1848, westward expansion became inevitable. Explorers, miners, traders, and ranchers flooded West, and a cross-country mail route started up between Saint Louis and San Francisco in 1857. The walls of one of the stage stations can still be seen near Pine Springs Campground. The Apaches, led by Geronimo, fought hard to retain their native lands during the Indian Wars of the late 1800s. The U.S. Army finally overpowered them in 1886, and the Apache were moved to a reservation in the nearby Sacramento Mountains. The Guadalupe Mountains are now a sanctuary for wildlife and human visitors alike.

Admirers of Anasazi architecture will find much to appreciate in the six ruins groups preserved at Hovenweep National Monument astride the Colorado-Utah border. Towers perched at the heads of sagebrush canyons are the work of master builders who farmed Cajon Mesa between A.D. 900 and 1300. The people who built these sturdy structures lived a life similar to the Anasazi at Mesa Verde thirty-five miles away.

By the tenth century, the Anasazi were living in apartment-style, masonry villages called pueblos. The majority of these pueblos were small units, which perhaps housed an extended family. Later, the people built multistoried dwellings in a variety of oval, circular, square, and "D" shapes on the edges of the canyons. Whereas Anasazi occupants of Mesa Verde built dwellings in sandstone cliff alcoves, the rock formations at Hovenweep do not contain such recesses. Instead, residents moved next to springs in canyon heads, where they dammed water flows behind rock terraces to irrigate their fields.

The stimulus of close-knit living brought about many technical and artistic advances in Anasazi culture. Their society became more powerful and organized, strong spiritual beliefs developed, and populations soared. Groups in search of good farmlands spilled out onto mesas all over the Four Corners area. Spring and fall equinoxes signaled the time for ceremonies to ensure good crops. Such activities were fundamental parts of pueblo life. Talented artisans made beautiful pottery, used for storage and cooking, or traded for turquoise, salt, copper, feathers, shells, and food.

Life in the Hovenweep area was sometimes quite difficult. Cyclic drought took its toll. Competition for dwindling natural resources and population pressures also added to the problem. By the late thirteenth century, Hovenweep's residents began to abandon the area and move south. They probably joined other Anasazi migrating to the Rio Grande and Little Colorado River drainages of New Mexico and Arizona, where their descendants live today.

Hovenweep's architectural wonders were first publicized by a Mormon settler en route to Utah in 1854. Twenty years later, another visitor gave the area the name Hovenweep, a Ute Indian word meaning "deserted valley." In 1917–1918, Smithsonian archeologist Dr. Jesse W. Fewkes, known for his work at Mesa Verde, conducted the first survey of the ruins and recommended that they be federally protected. In 1923 Hovenweep became a national monument.

Hovenweep Castle.

Anasazi handprints.

The best preserved and most accessible ruins are located at Square Tower, which includes the impressive Hovenweep Castle, a thick-walled structure with towers, as well as Rimrock and Stronghold houses. Archeological excavation has been limited here. Many structures have collapsed into mounds of rubble due to weathering and human impact. Visitors enter the ruins via a system of foot trails. Please treat the ruins with care. Do not climb on the walls or remove artifacts.

VISITOR INFORMATION

1.2 sq. mi. Ranger station at Square Tower open 8 A.M. to 4:30 P.M.: exhibits, information, bookstore. Although the monument is open year-round, roads are often impassable during and after bad weather; check local conditions before setting out. Self-guided trail at Square Tower. Inquire at ranger station about other ruins in monument. A 31-site campground is situated near ranger station. No group campsites. Supplies available at Hatch or Ismay trading posts. Motel accommodations in Blanding and Bluff, Utah, and Cortez, Colorado. For more information, write: Superintendent, Hovenweep National Monument, McElmo Rt., Cortez, CO 81321; or telephone (303) 529-4465 (Mesa Verde National Park). www.nps.gov/hove

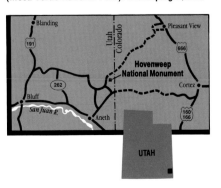

HUBBELL TRADING POST NATIONAL HISTORIC SITE

Hubbell rug room.

VISITOR INFORMATION

160 acres. Open 8 A.M. to 6:30 P.M. (summer); closed Thanksgiving, Christmas, and New Year's Day. Visitor center: rug weaving and silversmithing demonstrations, bookstore, exhibits. Regular tours of Hubbell Home and self-guided tour of homestead. Traditional crafts and supplies offered for sale by Southwest Parks and Monuments Association in trading post. No camping. Picnicking allowed. Lodging and food at Ganado, Window Rock, and Chinle. Trading post is en route to Canyon de Chelly, Grand Canyon, Petrified Forest, and Hopi Mesas. Note: Navajo Reservation observes daylight saving time, the remainder of Arizona off reservation does not. For more information, write: Superintendent, Hubbell Trading Post National Historic Site, Box 150, Ganado, AZ 86505; or telephone (520) 755-3475. www.nps.gov/hutr For more information on Navajo rugs: navajorugs.spma.org

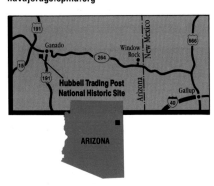

John Lorenzo Hubbell, given the title Don Lorenzo because of his Spanish blood, arrived in eastern Arizona from New Mexico around 1873. Keen to take advantage of the new wool markets opening in the East, Hubbell established a trading post at Ganado Lake in 1876, moving to an existing trading post at the present location two years later. Hubbell's main customers were Navajos, native people returning to a large, new, government-created reservation in the area after four years of federal incarceration in southeastern New Mexico.

As Western frontiers continued to open, sensitive individuals like Hubbell were important catalysts in healing distrust and hard feelings between Indians and Anglos caused by encounters with Spaniards, Mexican settlers, and the U.S. Army. Hubbell Trading Post has been preserved as a national historic site since 1965, but it remains an active trading post and an important meeting place between cultures.

Don Lorenzo, known initially to the Navajo as "Double Glasses," and later as *Naakaii Saani*, or Old Mexican, was the son of a Spanish mother and American father. Soon after moving to Ganado, he married Lina Rubi, a Spanish woman, in St. Johns, Arizona. They subsequently raised two daughters and two sons; the sons later took over the family business. The *Diné*, as the Navajo call themselves, had long traded with other native people and welcomed new markets now available to them in New Mexico and farther east. They bartered their sheep for prized Anglo supplies like flour, sugar, coffee, canned goods, tobacco, tools, and cloth. The sale of alcohol on the reservation was illegal, and Hubbell made a great effort to protect the native population from such vices.

Hubbell built up the trading post at Ganado with the aid of C. N. Cotton, his partner between 1884 and 1889. The partnership also allowed him to concentrate on expanding his trading empire, eventually establishing twenty-four trading posts. He encouraged the Navajo to return to weaving larger blankets of traditional design and had many examples of the best designs reproduced as paintings. The renowned Ganado blankets, with their distinctive deep red color and cross motifs, along with Two Gray Hills, Crystal, Chinle, and other local designs, are still bought and sold at the trading post today. In 1890, Hubbell also hired a Mexican artisan to teach silver jewelry making to the Indians. What we now consider traditional Navajo crafts owe much of their popularity to Hubbell's initiative.

The 160-acre Hubbell homestead includes a barn and corrals. At its peak, the Hubbell Trading Post employed wagon drivers, cooks, blacksmiths, a gardener who grew fruits and vegetables, and field hands. Any excess goods were traded at the post or sent to other markets. Next to the trading post is the 1901 Hubbell home, a large, well-built adobe house with high ceilings supported by pine vigas, or beams. The house reflects northwestern New Mexican architecture, very typically Hispanic. A 1934 stone guest hogan, or traditional Navajo house—a memorial to Hubbell— sits beside the house. Atop a hill across the wash is the family cemetery.

Don Lorenzo was an avid collector, and the Hubbell home boasts a fabulous array of Indian baskets, huge Navajo rugs, drawings and paintings by famous American artists, and a classic book collection. Hubbell welcomed travelers and, in 1913, entertained President Theodore Roosevelt, who was on his way to see the Hopi Snake Dance at Walpi. Having led a dynamic and satisfying life, Don Lorenzo died in 1930. He is still remembered by the Navajo as a trusted friend and advisor— one man who made a difference in the lives of many.

The trading post.

VISITOR INFORMATION

274 sq. mi. Alan Bible Visitor Center in Boulder City is open daily, except Thanksgiving, Christmas, and New Year's days; 8:30 A.M. to 4:30 P.M. Offers exhibits, audiovisual program, interpretive activities, information, bookstore, and desert botanical garden display. 6 developed areas on Lake Mead and 3 on Lake Mohave have visitor facilities, including houseboat and equipment rental. Concessionaire-operated lodging includes 6 motels and 8 trailer parks. Camping at 8 National Park Service campgrounds on a first-come, first-served basis. Backcountry camping allowed. Activities include water sports, fishing, hiking, nature watching, scenic drives, picnicking. Hiking is a winter activity in this desert environment. Bring adequate water, sun protection, and topographical map for all hikes. Fishing license required for shore fishing; fishing license and special use stamp required from Arizona and Nevada for fishing from boat. Boaters check lake rules before launching. Guided tours of Hoover Dam and self-guided tours of Davis Dam offered by Bureau of Reclamation. Valley of Fire State Park, a 1.5-hour drive from Boulder City, highlights area geology and Indian petroglyphs. Lost City Museum in the town of Overton interprets Anasazi culture. For more information, write: Superintendent, Lake Mead National Recreational Area, 601 Nevada Highway, Boulder City, NV 89005-2426; or telephone (702) 293-8990. www.nps.gov/lame

Lake Mead from Grapevine Mesa.

Lake Mead came into existence in 1935, when the enormous bulk of Boulder Dam (later renamed Hoover Dam) began to tame the seasonal fluctuations of the mighty Colorado River for human water and power needs. Hoover Dam, which straddles Black Canyon near Boulder City, Nevada, remains one of this country's most impressive technological achievements. In 1953, Davis Dam was built downstream, and Lake Mohave was born. The two lakes and the surrounding rugged desert make up Lake Mead National Recreation Area. One hundred-and-ten-mile long Lake Mead offers something for almost any interest: boating, scuba diving, waterskiing, swimming, wind surfing, fishing, hiking, birdwatching, and touring the area's many historical sites.

The desert's distinctive appearance is the result of 600 million years of geologic and climatic changes. Although only four or five inches of rain now fall here annually, for 300 million years this landscape accommodated an inland sea. Marine organisms swimming in these warm waters died, their limy skeletons piling up into deposits thousands of feet deep. During a period of uplift 200 million years ago, the sea floor rose and the

(continued)

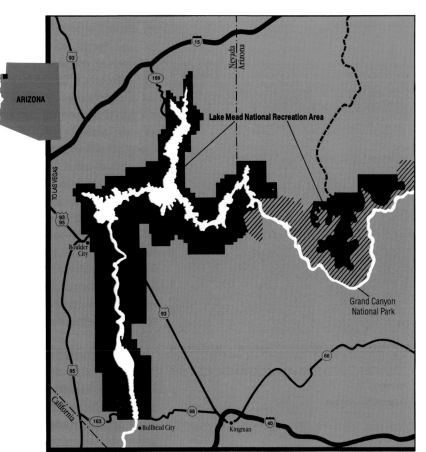

The marina at Katherine.

Desert bighorn sheep.

Beavertail cactus.

Petroglyphs, Grapevine Canyon.

interspersed with bursage, food for the bighorn sheep population. Shaggy Joshua trees signify the Mojave, and a particularly fine group can be seen on the road to Pearce Ferry, a nineteenth-century Mormon river crossing. Cacti are well adapted for life here in the desert, with their ability to store water for the dry months. Wildflowers have another strategy, their seeds lying dormant underground during dry periods, then germinating; surprising technicolor blooms burst out after winter and spring rains. In the cool evenings, the desert hops with jackrabbits, coyotes, ringtail cats, kangaroo rats, and kit foxes. Thick-skinned reptiles also live here, including poisonous rattlesnakes and Gila monsters, both of which should be left alone when encountered. Along windswept lakeshores, Fremont poplar and willow trees shelter noisy ducks, gulls, grebes, and white pelicans, which feed heartily on striped and largemouth bass, black crappie, rainbow trout, and catfish.

Around the time of Christ, after their people had passed thousands of years hunting and gathering throughout the desert, members of the Archaic Desert culture began to settle along the Colorado River and beside springs, where they grew corn, squash, beans, and melons. By A.D. 500, the Virgin River Anasazi were living in pit houses and making baskets and other artifacts. Within the next few centuries, groups were living in pueblos in the Overton area, where they built multilevel, masonry houses, developed beautiful pottery, and mined salt, as well as turquoise and other minerals used for paints. By A.D. 1200, this thriving culture had mysteriously disappeared, perhaps moving east to Arizona's Hopi Mesas. Their Lost City was inundated by Lake Mead, but a museum at Overton chronicles this prehistoric heritage.

When Spanish explorer Melchior Díaz discovered the area around present-day Katherine in 1540, nomadic Southern Paiutes lived in the region. The Spanish Crown then claimed ownership of this territory for the next 281 years; in late 1829, Jose Antonio Armijo traveled through southern Nevada and the Las Vegas Wash, establishing the Spanish Trail from Santa Fe to Los Angeles. In the mid-1800s, increasing numbers of Mormon settlers, military surveyors, miners, and traders filtered west. Gold, silver, and copper were mined extensively, and, as populations grew, a new riverboat service began to work the lower Colorado River, only to decline after the railroad reached here in 1877. Many early settlements became ghost towns, abandoned after mines were exhausted and the river dammed. Some of these sites are accessible only by boat, but others are located along scenic drives and trails.

sea became shallower. Evaporating seawater laid down salt deposits, and muddy tidal flats were crisscrossed by slow-moving streams carrying sandy sediments, which, along with gravel, logs, and branches washed down from high areas, mingled on top of existing sediments. These sediments eventually coalesced into rocks, distinguished by occasional petrified wood and striking pastel colors, the result of mineral oxidation in the rocks. Sixty million years later, hot, dry winds piled sand into great dunes, which are visible today as the swirling, ruddy Aztec Sandstone along the nature trail at Redstone Picnic Area on Northshore Road. This era was followed by a period of mountain building that wrenched deep-seated limestone up over younger rocks and formed great faults. The mountains were then subjected to erosion, a process still at work today.

Here in the northwestern corner of Arizona and the southern tip of Nevada, the Mojave, Sonoran, and Great Basin deserts meet. Because of this strategic location, the recreation area contains a diversity of plants and animals. Common in this arid environment are evenly spaced creosote bushes

MESA VERDE NATIONAL PARK

Cliff Palace.

There it was, occupying a great oval space under a grand cliff, wonderful to behold, appearing like an immense ruined castle with dismantled towers.

—Frederick Chapin, 1891
First published account of Cliff Palace

It may come as a surprise to those who think of the Western United States as newly settled to learn that the architects of Cliff Palace, a remarkably preserved prehistoric cliff dwelling in Mesa Verde National Park, inhabited this region from about 200 B.C. to A.D. 1300. Known by the Navajo word *Anasazi*, or "Ancient Ones," these talented, hardy people developed a complex culture that eventually became part of a greater tradition still alive in modern Southwestern pueblos. This lifestyle emphasized close-knit living in artfully constructed masonry buildings, farming, trade with other cultures, a strong religious tradition, and superb arts and crafts. Then, just as their culture seemed to reach its zenith, the Mesa Verdeans abandoned their pueblos. No one who visits Mesa Verde can fail to be intrigued by the story of this great culture and to consider what lessons the Anasazi have for us today.

Set amid the wild mesalands of southwest Colorado, Mesa Verde National Park preserves evidence of 800 years of Anasazi occupation. The Mesa Verde, literally "Green Table" in Spanish, supports abundant wildlife and enjoys eighteen inches of annual rainfall, undoubtedly one of the reasons the Anasazi originally settled here. By the sixth century, the Anasazi were firmly entrenched in a horticultural lifestyle. They cultivated squash, corn, and eventually beans on these mesas, but continued to hunt rabbits, deer, and other game and gather many wild foods, such as pinyon nuts, prickly pear cactus fruit, and Indian ricegrass. Yucca plants were some of the most useful, providing food, shampoo and, most important, fibers for sandals and baskets.

(continued)

VISITOR INFORMATION

80 sq. mi. Entrance fee. Open year-round, but winter weather may close roads; inquire at park entrance. Far View Visitor Center open 8 A.M. to 5 P.M. summer only: exhibits, interpretive activities, information, bookstore. Commercial tours of Chapin Mesa leave from Far View Lodge. Lodging, gas, and food available at Far View in summer only. For information and reservations call concessionaire at (970) 529-4421. Wetherill Mesa open in summer only: steep, 12-mile road leads to cliff dwellings and mesa-top ruins. Long House requires advance ticket purchase at Far View Visitor Center. Wetherill Mesa Road is open between 8 A.M. and 4:30 P.M. only.

Chapin Mesa is 21 miles from park entrance and contains many cliff dwellings and other ruins. Chapin Mesa Museum open 8 A.M. to 6:30 P.M. in summer, to 5 P.M. rest of year: exhibits, interpretive activities, information. 3 main cliff dwellings may be visited: Spruce Tree House is self-guided and free; Balcony House and Cliff Palace require advance ticket purchase at Far View Visitor Center. Tours of Spruce Tree House conducted in winter, weather permitting. Scenic Mesa Top Drives, with roadside interpretive exhibits, and views of cliff dwellings, open 8 A.M. to sunset in summer; may be closed to vehicles in winter, but open for snowshoeing or cross-country skiing. Snacks and gifts available year-round at Spruce Tree Terrace. Limited hiking trails available in the park. Check with a park ranger before any hiking. Morefield Village Campground near park entrance, open mid-April to October, has 477 campsites, available on a first-come, first-served basis. Groceries, take-out food, gas, and other supplies. Nearest towns are Cortez, Mancos, and Durango. Public transportation serves park. For more information, write: Superintendent, Mesa Verde National Park, Colorado 81330; or telephone (970) 529-4465 or 529-4475. www.nps.gov/meve

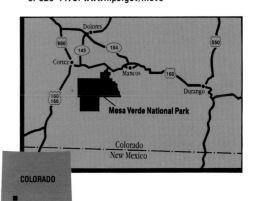

Kiva at Farview Ruin.

Doorway and kiva entrance, Spruce Tree House.

Acres of pinyon-juniper forest cover Mesa Verde, and gnarled Gambel oak and mountain mahogany thrive in exposed locations. On cooler, north-facing slopes forests of Douglas fir and ponderosa pine are common. Birds—from eagles to warblers—are common, and mule deer and coyotes are often seen scouting lower elevations of the mesas for food. Visitors are lucky if they glimpse elk or black bear. Reintroduced wild turkeys are increasingly seen feeding along the road into the park.

Three distinct periods of Anasazi culture have been identified in the park. Scattered throughout the mesas and canyons are the remains of subterranean, mud plaster-and-pole pit houses used by families of Basketmaker Anasazi and early Pueblo Anasazi between A.D. 550 and 900. Of the more than 4,000 sites discovered here, most are mesa-top villages, or pueblos, on Wetherill and Chapin mesas. Larger pueblos developed between A.D. 900 and 1075, and crop cultivation became more intense. In this transitional period, aboveground, apartment-style buildings were built from sandstone and mortar to house a burgeoning population. Fine pottery making and rock art perhaps reflected a growing emphasis on aesthetics and ceremonial activities, and former pit houses were frequently transformed into kivas, places for ceremonial gatherings.

Populations peaked in the final period of occupation at Mesa Verde, dating from A.D. 1075 to 1300. Towns of greater complexity were now necessary, featuring multistory, many-chambered structures built around a central plaza. The Anasazi very likely faced many problems we are familiar with in the twentieth century: overpopulation, changing climatic patterns that affected crops, exhaustion of natural resources, and competition for remaining supplies. In the 1200s many Mesa Verdeans moved to live full time in the sheltered cliffs, building sophisticated towns in natural alcoves in the sandstone canyon walls.

They used handholds in the rock to reach their mesa-top farm plots. Available rainfall normally was adequate for crop cultivation, but in dry years catchment dams, which retained pockets of soil, were used as a fallback for growing crops. The Anasazi lifestyle took its physical toll in a life expectancy of only thirty-two to thirty-four years and a tendency toward diseases like arthritis. The diet, which may have been deficient in iron due to the quantity of corn consumed, was likely a contributing factor. Finally, a severe twenty-three-year drought seems to have been the final straw for residents of the Four Corners. The "Ancient Ones" of Mesa Verde abandoned their cliff dwellings and moved south among the pueblos of the Rio Grande and Little Colorado basins.

Mesa Verde's splendid cliff dwellings lay undisturbed until the 1880s, when they were publicized by a Mancos ranching family, the Wetherills. Richard Wetherill became a famous amateur archeologist, going on to lead archeological expeditions into Grand Gulch and Chaco Canyon. Mesa Verde's rich legacy was preserved when the area received national park status in 1906. In recognition of its unique place in history, the park was designated a United Nations World Heritage site in 1978.

Original wall decorations in tower of Cliff Palace.

Mesa Verde black-on-white bowl.

Early settlers in central Arizona's Verde Valley were so convinced that the imposing five-story ruin nestled high in a cliff alcove above Beaver Creek was built by Aztec leader Montezuma that they named it Montezuma Castle, and this "castle" does indeed seem to be worthy of a mighty leader. But its true architects were, in fact, farmers of the Sinagua culture who migrated here from the northern high country in the twelfth century. In this valley, their story is linked to that of the Hohokam, desert people from the south who had skillfully farmed the valley for centuries, and to neighboring trading cultures like the Anasazi.

Montezuma Castle is one of the best-preserved Indian ruins in the country. Nearby Castle A—a large dwelling on the scale of Montezuma Castle—has collapsed, while most of Montezuma Castle's original limestone walls and twenty rooms remain intact after 700 years.

The fertile Verde Valley plain allowed Sinagua farmers to grow corn, squash, beans, and cotton, like their neighbors the Hohokam. The Sinagua were traditionally dryland farmers, as their Spanish name meaning "without water" implies. Here, however, they irrigated their fields with water from adjacent Beaver Creek. Just north of Montezuma Castle is Montezuma Well, a detached unit of the national monument. This limestone sinkhole is filled with water from a natural spring. It was used by both Sinagua and Hohokam for irrigation, and lime-encrusted remnants of their irrigation ditches are visible today. Pit houses and aboveground masonry dwellings surround the well, underscoring the importance of this water source to prehistoric valley residents. An excavated, twelfth-century Hohokam pit house—a rarity in the national park system—is on view here.

The Sinagua and Hohokam were part of an important trading network that brought other cultures through this natural north-south corridor. Valley residents bartered their plentiful food, cotton, and local salt for macaws, shell, turquoise, and fine cooking and storage pots. The Sinagua tended to locate their small villages and storage rooms along natural cliff terraces, or they walled up the mouths of caves. Originally pit house dwellers, the Sinagua may have picked up their masonry skills from Anasazi people who settled in the Flagstaff area after the eruption of Sunset Crater in 1064–1065. The Anasazi and Hohokam were both village dwellers and had developed effective water catchment systems, which the Sinagua found useful. But their own expertise in working stone and bone into implements, as well as weaving cotton cloth, provided useful articles for daily living.

So attractive was this eden that other Sinagua refugees from the north began to flood here in the 1100s and 1200s. This population explosion may have caused friction between the new immigrants and the existing residents. Later buildings have the look of fortified dwellings, but whether this was intentional is still unclear. By the time Spaniard Antonio de Espejo rode through Verde Valley in 1583, the Sinagua and Hohokam had disappeared, and the only residents were hunter-gatherer Yavapai Indians. Evidence is strong but inconclusive that some of the Sinagua may have drifted north in the 1400s to join Hopi and Zuni pueblos.

Archeologists began excavating in the Verde Valley in the late 1800s, after the railroad and settlers had focused attention on the treasures here. A U.S. Army naturalist at Fort Verde mapped and dug many ruins, including Montezuma Castle, in 1884. Eight years later, Cosmos Mindeleff surveyed the valley for the U.S. Bureau of Ethnology and theorized that its twelfth-century settlers had come from the north. A colleague, Jesse W. Fewkes, followed him here in 1895 and 1906 with the intention of collecting specimens and proving the Hopi legend that this was their ancestral land. President Theodore Roosevelt proclaimed Montezuma Castle a national monument in 1906.

Montezuma Castle.

VISITOR INFORMATION

Approximately 1.3 sq. mi. Entrance fee. Montezuma Well, 11 miles northeast, no fee. Open year-round; 8 A.M. to 7 P.M. (summer), 8 A.M. to 5 P.M. (winter). Visitor center: exhibits, interpretive activities, information, bookstore. Self-guided trail passes by Montezuma Castle, but due to fragile state of ruin, entry is prohibited. Picnicking is allowed at Montezuma Castle and Montezuma Well, but no other services within monument. Nearest facilities are in Camp Verde 5 miles away. Scenic Verde Valley offers hiking, backpacking, and camping in national forest. Private campgrounds available. Advance reservations for national forest campsites are recommended in summer; call 1-877-444-6777. Tuzigoot National Monument is 25 miles west. For more information, write: Superintendent, Montezuma Castle National Monument, P.O. Box 219, Camp Verde, AZ 86322; or telephone (520) 567-3322. www.nps.gov/moca

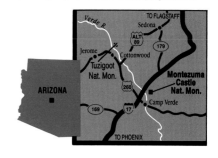

NATURAL BRIDGES NATIONAL MONUMENT

Owachomo Bridge.

Horsecollar Ruin in White Canyon.

VISITOR INFORMATION

Approximately 11.9 sq. mi. Open all year. Entrance fee collected March to October. Visitor center open 9 A.M. to 4:30 P.M., extended summer hours: information, exhibits, interpretive programs. Bridges are about 3.5 mi. apart at canyon bottom. To view bridges, take Bridge View Drive (9 miles one way), providing overlooks into canyon, or hike 9-mile loop trail in canyon. Picnic area and 13 campsites at campground. No services. Nearest facilities in Blanding, 40 miles east. For more information, write: Superintendent, Natural Bridges National Monument, Box 1, Lake Powell, UT 84533-0101; or telephone (435) 692-1234. www.nps.gov/nabr

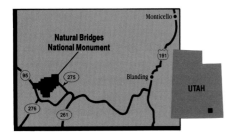

Deep within the White and Armstrong canyons of Cedar Mesa in southeastern Utah, Natural Bridges National Monument protects three spectacular sandstone natural bridges carved by side streams of the Colorado River, as well as fine examples of prehistoric Indian ruins and rock art. One of these spans—Sipapu—is second in size only to nearby Rainbow Bridge, the world's largest known natural bridge.

The flat-topped bridges were first seen by white men in 1883, when prospector Cass Hite and several companions entered the canyons with a Paiute Indian guide. Strong public interest led to the bridges and adjacent Indian ruins being designated a national monument in 1908. A government survey led by William B. Douglass that year studied the bridges, the well-preserved prehistoric artwork on them, and Indian remnants dotting the canyons. Douglass gave the spans their Hopi names, concluding that the prehistoric residents, the Anasazi, were ancestors of the present-day Hopi, living 120 miles to the south. The largest bridge, Sipapu, with its portal-like appearance, reminded Douglass of the *sipapu*, or Gateway of Life, in Hopi kivas. The second span, Kachina, bears pictographs associated with Hopi gods, or *kachinas*. A protrusion atop the third bridge, slender Owachomo, led to its name, meaning "rock mound."

The bridges here are formed of Cedar Mesa Sandstone, originally crossbedded Permian sand dunes. Natural bridges are carved by stream flow, as opposed to forces of wind and ice, which form arches. Ten million years ago, side streams to the infant Colorado River followed a meandering path along the gentle curves of the land. But uplift and tilting of the Colorado Plateau caused the rivers to cut down into the bedrock, forming canyons. The canyons' looping meanders, known as "goosenecks," slowed the periodic floods that engulfed the canyons. But the swollen streams and accompanying rock debris began grinding away at these obstructions, finally drilling an exit to the other side, shortcutting the stream path. As the holes grew, natural bridges formed. Wind, rain, and water then smoothed out the curves of the bridges—a never-ending process. In time, however, bridges crack under their own weight, slabs of rock fall off, and eventually they collapse.

Anasazi Indians used these sheltered, well-watered canyons from approximately A.D. 100 to 1300. Early Basketmaker Anasazi grew maize on mesa tops and canyon ledges, hunted game, gathered wild crops, and wove baskets and clothing from cliff rose and yucca fibers. As time wore on, they made pottery and also began to grow beans. They congregated in small pueblos of multi-roomed structures centered around a plaza and kiva, of which Horsecollar Ruin is the largest and most sophisticated here.

In Natural Bridges, mountain lions track mule deer, and bobcats, coyotes, and shy desert kit foxes, at home in the pinyon-juniper forest and brush of the mesa top, enjoy a smorgasbord of rabbits, hares, and rodents. Reptiles, including collared lizards and the occasional rattlesnake, sun themselves on canyon slopes, among pockets of mountain mahogany, Gambel oak, and serviceberry. Overhead wheel ravens and magpies and darting white-throated swifts, as well as raptors like golden eagles, falcons, and hawks. After a storm, potholes in the local "slickrock" fill with water, hosting swarms of insects and spadefoot toads, which patiently await this opportunity to reproduce in the pools.

Time spent here is well rewarded. Although a paved road leads to overlooks of the bridges and their fascinating surroundings, a stroll along the hiking trails is recommended for a different perspective on the monument.

Some of the largest and best-preserved cliff dwellings in the nation are protected at Navajo National Monument, hidden among the sandstone canyons of Arizona's Navajo Reservation. The architects of these lofty homes were the Kayenta Anasazi, a major branch of the Anasazi of the Four Corners region. They had lived in the Tsegi Canyon–Marsh Pass area for centuries, when in the mid-1200s, they were beset by increasing drought and shrinking natural resources. Perhaps in desperation, they moved to the protected cliff alcoves of Tsegi Canyon, built pueblos on the precarious ledges, and continued farming canyon bottoms. From about A.D. 1250 to A.D. 1300, they eked out an existence in Tsegi Canyon (a Navajo name generally translated as "rock canyon"), finally admitting defeat and apparently scattering to the Hopi Mesas, where some of their descendants still live. Navajo National Monument's Betatakin and Keet Seel cliff dwellings are poignant reminders of a resourceful culture.

Named by the Navajo Indians who settled in the area in the mid- to late 1800s, or perhaps earlier, Betatakin, meaning "ledge house," and Keet Seel, meaning "broken pieces of pottery," were begun in the A.D. 1250s by a few adventurous Kayenta Anasazi families. Those at Betatakin were joined in 1267 by a few other advance groups who began to stockpile timber to build housing for the large group of settlers that followed in 1275. Due to the sloping bedrock floor of the cave, Betatakin had to be supported on a foundation of "wall-footing grooves" and shored up with mud for greater stability. A retaining wall was built, behind which graded earth provided a level walkway for residents. Rock art here includes bighorn sheep, as well as the Hopi Fire Clan symbol, leading some Hopis to claim this as an ancestral site; they call it Kawestima, or "North Village." Betatakin can be viewed from Sandal Trail close to the visitor center or reached by a scheduled five-mile hike with a ranger.

Keet Seel, requiring a permit and a challenging overland hike or guided horseback trip of sixteen miles round-trip, was occupied through earlier intervals than Betatakin. It is the larger and more impressive of the two ruins open to public scrutiny. A third, the architecturally dissimilar Inscription House, is closed due to its unstable condition and access problems. Tree-ring dating of wood beams has shown that Keet Seel was founded in A.D. 950 by groups whose earlier homes here were probably destroyed by the later "Tsegi phase" builders of about A.D. 1250 to 1286. During construction of the new pueblo in 1250, some of the timber from these earlier residences was apparently reused. The estimated 150 people who

Betatakin.

lived at Keet Seel in its heyday were more mobile than the people of Betatakin. This seems to be reflected in the wide range of influences felt in their architecture. As drought persisted and arroyo erosion continued, people moved away, allowing extra rooms to be converted to storage. When the pueblo was finally abandoned, the people sealed their granaries, perhaps intending to return when the climate improved.

In 1895, Richard Wetherill was guided to Keet Seel, probably by local Navajos. Wetherill was a rancher and amateur archeologist who was among the first white men to visit the cliff dwellings of Mesa Verde. Later, in 1909, his brother, John, and Professor Byron Cummings of the University of Utah were the first outsiders to be led by a local Navajo guide to see Betatakin, just after Keet Seel had been protected as Navajo National Monument.

Like Canyon de Chelly, which also contains Anasazi ruins and is surrounded by the Navajo Reservation, Navajo National Monument juxtaposes two completely different Indian cultures. Here, the contemporary life of the Navajo, emphasizing livestock grazing and fine handicrafts, is no less fascinating than that of the Anasazi.

VISITOR INFORMATION

360 acres. Monument is remote, but the entrance road is paved and open year-round; visitor center open 8 A.M. to 6 P.M. in summer, 8 A.M. to 4:30 P.M. in winter, closed Thanksgiving, Christmas, and New Year's Day: audiovisual programs, bookstore. Guided tours of both ruins from May to September only, but 1-mile round trip, self-guided Sandal Trail provides dramatic view of Betatakin Ruin. Permit required for 16-mile roundtrip hike to Keet Seel (limited to 20 visitors per day); horseback tours with Navajo guide can also be arranged at the visitor center. Call for updated tour and facility information. 30 campsites and group campground near visitor center (closed mid-October through mid-April; primitive campground near Keet Seel. No food, gas, or lodging at monument, but full services available in Kayenta, 28 miles northeast of monument headquarters. The Navajo Reservation is on daylight saving time in summer, in contrast to the rest of Arizona. For more information, write: Superintendent, Navajo National Monument, HC-71, Box 3, Tonalea, AZ 86044-9704; or telephone (520) 672-2366/2367. www.nps.gov/nava

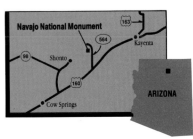

ORGAN PIPE CACTUS NATIONAL MONUMENT

The Ajo Mountains.

VISITOR INFORMATION

516 sq. mi. Entrance fee. Open year-round. Visitor center open 8 A.M. to 5 P.M. daily: audiovisual programs, exhibits, interpretive activities, information, bookstore. 2 winding scenic drives on graded dirt roads: 21-mile Ajo Mountain Drive and 53-mile Puerto Blanco Drive—not recommended for motorhomes over 25 feet or for trailers. Several unimproved backcountry roads lead to historic ranches, mines, and other sights; inquire first about conditions. 6 hiking trails of varying lengths, including 1 from visitor center; backcountry hiking requires careful planning to avoid getting lost. Summers are very hot and can be wet; scenic roads may be washed out. Winter temperatures are more comfortable. Campground has 208 campsites on first-come, first-served basis. Backcountry camping also allowed with permit. Nearest visitor services at Lukeville, Why, Ajo, and in Sonoyta, Mexico. Note: Check with U.S. Customs officials at Lukeville about regulations before crossing U.S.–Mexico border. For more information, write: Superintendent, Organ Pipe Cactus National Monument, Route 1, Box 100, Ajo, AZ 85321; or telephone (520) 387-6849. www.nps.gov/orpi

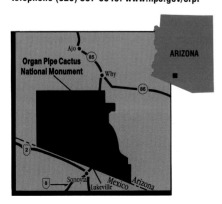

Newcomers to Arizona's Sonoran Desert may be forgiven for thinking that this strange landscape is like an infinite dry ocean, strewn here and there with mountain islands rising above the heat haze. Yet the Sonoran Desert, preserved here in the 516 square miles of Organ Pipe Cactus National Monument, teems with wildlife of such diversity that the area was designated an International Biosphere Reserve in 1976. Not only does the monument contain great stands of organ pipe cactus, which is rarely found north of the Mexican border, but its geographical range allows representatives of three distinctive Sonoran Desert habitats to coexist within its boundaries. Visitors can enjoy this special region by taking two long scenic drives through the monument, by hiking trails of varying difficulty, or by camping in the monument's year-round campground.

Organ Pipe is home to tall mountains flanked by gravelly slopes known as *bajadas*, great plains, dry washes, and salt flats. As the scenery changes so too do the many plant communities growing in the different areas, a fact fully appreciated by the desert creatures. The hot, dry Lower Colorado Desert environment found in the western section sizzles under summer temperatures that often exceed 105 degrees Fahrenheit. Hardy creosote bush and bursage tough out the extremes in the valleys, while a mixture of scrub and palo verde characterizes the dry, volcanic slopes of nearby mountains. Few plants can tolerate the salty valley bordering Mexico; the aptly named saltbush seems almost the only taker. Nocturnal kangaroo rats are specially adapted to survive the

heat and lack of water, as are large-eared jackrabbits, and both generally remain out of sight until twilight in hot summer months. In the daytime, they and reptiles like lizards, desert tortoises, and the western diamondback rattlesnake burrow into cool sand or lie motionless under a shady bush. Coyotes, bighorn sheep, and hawks venture out in the day, but wisely restrict most of their food searches to cooler morning and evening temperatures.

Organ pipe cactus in bloom.

The moister Arizona Uplands farther east allow a much wider array of desert-adapted plants to thrive. A mixture of palo verde and ocotillo, as well as organ pipe, saguaro, teddybear cholla, and prickly pear cacti prefer the bajadas beside the Puerto Blanco and Ajo mountains. Gila woodpeckers, elf owls, and other small birds seek out the tall, pipe-shaped saguaro as a sheltering home, while piglike javelinas rely in part on prickly pear cactus for water. Like most cacti, the thick-skinned organ pipe has sharp spines to cool and protect it. A network of roots allows it to take advantage of fierce summer rainstorms, storing away water in gelatinous tissues. Abundant sunlight enables the cactus to photosynthesize water and carbon dioxide into food, and a preference for south-facing locations offers some protection from deadly winter frosts.

During years of adequate rainfall, gold poppies, lupines, and pink owl clover delight the eye with their show in early spring. They are joined soon after by glorious cactus blossoms. During this extravagant display, long-nosed bats come to drink cactus nectar and unwittingly pollinate their hosts as they brush by. By late summer, luscious fruits appear as tempting food for white-winged doves and other desert dwellers. In nature's endless cycle, discarded seeds will take hold in the soil, perhaps shaded by palo verde trees, and young cactus plants will join aging relatives. Deeper in the Ajo Mountains, shady, well-watered canyons shelter stands of jojoba, agave, rosewood, and juniper. Prehistoric desert people, related to the Papago of the Sonoran Desert, sought such cool spots seasonally to gather wild foods and to drink from pools of water in the rock known as *tinajas*. Along the Mexican border grow elephant trees, limberbush, and senita cacti, Sonoran Desert species mostly found farther south in Mexico.

Over the centuries, Spanish, Mexican, and American settlers joined the Papago (the Tohono O'odham) in the Sonoran Desert. Dryland farming gave way in the late nineteenth century to cattle ranching and mining of the desert's precious metals. Once a disturbed natural habitat, the area within the monument is now reverting to wilderness.

Tinajas in the Ajo Mountains.

Pack rat.

Hohokam petroglyph.

Desert hairy scorpion.

Organ pipe and cholla cacti, Senita Basin.

PECOS
NATIONAL HISTORICAL PARK

*The mission church
and wall of pueblo ruin.*

VISITOR INFORMATION

**Approximately 10.2 sq. mi. Entrance fee. Open
8 A.M. to 5 P.M. Labor Day–Memorial Day, until
6 P.M. Memorial Day–Labor Day. Visitor center:
audiovisual programs, museum exhibits, information, bookstore. Self-guiding ruins trail. No
camping. Picnicking permitted. Food and lodging
available in Santa Fe or Las Vegas. No public
transportation to park. For more information, write:
Superintendent, Pecos National Historical Park,
P.O. Box 418, Pecos, NM 87552; or telephone
(505) 757-6032. www.nps.gov/peco**

Doorway in church.

At first sight, the great church ruin at Pecos in north-central New Mexico, with its thick walls soaring above several low hills, seems merely to continue the fascinating story of the Spanish missionary effort in New Mexico. But those insignificant-seeming mounds are, in fact, the remains of the mighty Indian pueblo of Pecos, for several centuries one of a handful of important pueblo trading centers straddling the gateway to the eastern plains.

When archeologist Alfred V. Kidder explored these ruins between 1915 and 1929, the more than 16,000 Indian and Spanish artifacts he found (many exhibited in the park's visitor center) provided evidence of a remarkable culture at Pecos between the twelfth and nineteenth centuries.

Abundant natural resources attracted migrant hunters and gatherers here for thousands of years before pueblos grew up. Eventually, agricultural experimentation led to settlement around the Pecos area. Pit houses dating to the A.D. 800s mark this period. Early in the twelfth century Anasazi settlers, driven from the arid area to the northwest, apparently joined existing groups in the Rio Grande area. The Anasazi undoubtedly had a major influence on the inhabitants of the Pecos Valley, for the valley people began to coalesce into multistory pueblos, of which Pecos became the most powerful.

At its zenith, when Coronado's Spanish conquistadors viewed it in 1540, Cicuyé, as the Spaniards first called Pecos, was an impressive sight. A veritable fortress, it rose four to five stories high and sheltered 2,000 people. Trade between Pueblo and Plains Indians was the lifeblood of Pecos. Apaches camped beneath the walls, barter-ing buffalo skins and meat for flint, pottery, pinyon nuts, turquoise, and cloth. Pecos's location linked the Rio Grande pueblos with the plains, making it a vital cultural center. But the newly arrived Spanish horsemen, initially welcomed into their midst, would shortly change the lives of the people of Pecos forever.

Finding no fabled gold north of the border, Coronado retreated to Mexico. But in 1598, the Spaniards returned with a new goal: to establish missions and convert the Pueblo Indians to Christianity. The largest of four mission churches at this site was finished by Franciscan Father Andrés Juarez by 1625; its foundations lie beneath the present church ruin, which dates from 1717.

During the mission period, trade at the adjoining pueblo grew to provide goods to "pay tribute" to the Spanish Crown. By the mid-1600s drought, European diseases, famine, exhausted resources, and suppression of native spiritual beliefs led the Pueblos to revolt in 1680. The missions were destroyed, and the Spaniards were forced south. The Pecos people reclaimed their heritage and defiantly built a kiva in the ruins of the *convento*, the living quarters of the mission.

Following the Spanish Reconquest in 1692, new problems overtook Pecos. Bold Comanche warriors astride European horses raided frequently. Disease was still rampant. The population of Pecos had dropped to 200 by the time peace was made with the Comanches in 1786. Spanish settlers moved down the river and established a trading center that focused attention away from the Indian pueblo. By the time Mexico won its independence from Spain in 1821, the once-unconquered pueblo of Pecos barely existed. In 1838, the remaining seventeen people at Pecos moved to Jemez Pueblo on the other side of the Jemez Mountains, possibly because the people there spoke a similar language.

Pecos became a national monument in 1965, and a national historical park in 1990. The 5,500-acre Forked Lightning Ranch, many arche-ological sites, ruts of the Santa Fe Trail, two historic buildings, and several miles of the Pecos River were added to the park in 1991. The Glorieta Unit was added in November 1990 to commemo-rate two Civil War battle sites.

*Colorado four-
o'clock.*

PETRIFIED FOREST NATIONAL PARK

Some national parks hint at their treasures before you actually get to the park entrance, but Petrified Forest in northeastern Arizona betrays almost nothing of its hidden wonders to passersby on the interstate. Yet this special place preserves the largest known accumulation of petrified logs in the world; fossils of long-extinct, late Triassic plants and animals sheathed in soft rock; the soft pastel wilderness of the Painted Desert; and the scattered artifacts of people who lived here for more than 3,000 years.

This arid high desert was once a humid, equatorial floodplain, crisscrossed by rivers flowing toward an ancient coastline to the west. But according to the plate tectonic theory, 225 million years ago, in the late Triassic period, North America was not far from West Africa. When the supercontinent of Pangaea separated into distinct continents, what is now North America broke free and gradually moved northwestward. Ongoing climatic and geologic changes prompted nature into a frenzy of experimentation to adapt to these conditions. Amphibians gave way to strange reptiles, lorded over by the phytosaur, a fearsome crocodile-like creature that attacked on land and in water. Later, small primitive dinosaurs began appearing. Lungfish and snails populated the swampy rivers, and tangled fernlike cycads and 100- to 200-foot conifers lined the riverbanks.

Most of these giant trees grew outside the area of the present-day park. As they toppled, they washed down rivers into logjams, became saturated by water, and were rapidly buried under many feet of silt, which cut off oxygen and delayed decay. Clouds of ash from volcanoes to the south blew in and blanketed the ground. Silicates mixed with groundwater seeped into the cells of the buried tree trunks, forming hard quartz crystals that effectively petrified these arboreal giants. Many trees were filled with beautifully colored quartz crystals (jasper, amethyst, and smoky quartz). Eventually, the silt and sand washed in by streams formed the shales and sandstones known today as the Chinle Formation. (It is the many-layered, multicolored Chinle that gives character to this desert panorama.) Millions of years later, the gem-filled tree trunks were buried still deeper by a layer of marine sediments and lava, the Bidahochi Formation, which covered the Chinle rock. The remains of the Bidahochi can be seen at the highest point in the park along the Painted Desert rim and at Pilot Rock.

The climate has dried to a present-day average nine inches of annual precipitation. The rivers and seas have disappeared, and uplift of the Colorado Plateau has exposed the Chinle clays to erosion by water and wind. The badlands so vividly

Petrified trees at Long Logs.

Petrified wood.

evidenced at Blue Mesa and the Teepees are a product of merciless weathering of soft rock. It is erosion, too, that finally uncovered the long-buried petrified wood on view in the Jasper and Crystal forests, and at Long Logs in the park's southern reaches. Erosion of soft clay around the base of the logs has left many perched on pedestals, looking like benches for some weary giant. Eventually, they will fall to the ground, and the process will begin anew. At Agate Bridge, a huge petrified trunk spans an arroyo, poised to plunge at some future time.

The Petrified Forest story has an important human component, too. Desert Archaic people and Basketmaker and Pueblo Anasazi lived here from 1050 B.C. to A.D. 1400, progressing from scattered

(continued)

VISITOR INFORMATION

Approximately 147 sq. mi. Entrance fee. Open 7:30 A.M. to 5 P.M. in winter, longer rest of year. Park facilities may be closed on Christmas Day and New Year's; check in advance. Road sometimes closed by snow in winter. Park may be entered from I-40 or U.S. 180. Painted Desert Visitor Center (north entrance): audiovisual program, exhibits, interpretive activities, information, bookstore. These are also available at Rainbow Forest Museum (south entrance). Historic Painted Desert Inn Museum at Kachina Point has exhibits. 27-mile drive through park with pullouts for views and short hikes. Main petrified wood "forests" are in south. Picnic areas at Chinde Point and Rainbow Forest. 2 wilderness areas for cross-country hiking and backpack camping require permit and careful planning. Summers are very hot, and sudden storms frequently cause flashflooding. Check conditions and come prepared with adequate water and appropriate clothing. No developed campgrounds in park; nearest lodging and full services in Holbrook. Gifts, food, and gas at Painted Desert Oasis and Rainbow Forest Curios. For more information, write: Superintendent, Petrified Forest National Park, P.O. Box 2217, Petrified Forest, AZ 86028; or telephone (520) 524-6228. www.nps.gov/pefo

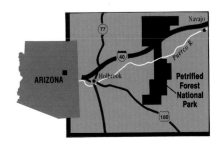

The Painted Desert.

Black-tailed jackrabbit.

Indian paintbrush.

Coyote tracks.

Petrified logs, Blue Mesa.

campsites, to pit house dwellings, to the 100-room pueblo along the Puerco River. The Indians hunted, gathered, and eventually farmed like other contemporary Anasazi; however, the Petrified Forest region was on a cultural frontier, between the Mogollon to the south, the Anasazi to the north, and other wandering Southwestern groups. Exchange of ideas undoubtedly occurred, as well as trade of petrified wood for food, pottery, and items like shells from the Pacific coast. The Anasazi made tools from petrified wood and even built dwellings with it, as seen at Agate House. Puerco Pueblo was occupied until about 1400, much later than many other Anasazi ruins found in the Four Corners region. The thirteenth-century drought apparently forced people to relocate close to the Puerco River, where they probably built farming terraces. When they were finally forced to leave they did so systematically, taking their belongings, perhaps moving to the Hopi Mesas to the northwest or to the pueblos east and west of the area. In time, the Navajo moved into the vacated land, where they remain today.

The first written account of petrified wood here came from Captain Lorenzo Sitgreaves, a U.S. Army surveyor sent in 1851 to map the new territory won by the United States from Mexico. While not being particularly impressed by the lonely landscape, he and his officers were nonetheless delighted by the haul of gems they pried from petrified logs. Their stories sparked great interest, and tourism grew. With the advent of the Santa Fe Railroad in 1882, boxcarloads of petrified wood began to be shipped back east for ornamental use. Adam and Anna Hanna opened a small inn at Adamana and offered guided tours of the area. In 1895, concerned local residents began to lobby for protection of Chalcedony Park, as it was then called. With a push from John Muir, who pressed his friend President Theodore Roosevelt for preservation, several petrified forests were protected in 1906 as Petrified Forest National Monument. The Painted Desert Inn was built in 1924 close to the monument to accommodate travelers on Route 66; it is now a National Historic Landmark within the park. Blue Mesa was added in 1930, Painted Desert followed two years later, and in 1970 two wilderness areas were established—the first in the national park system. In 1962, the monument was redesignated a national park.

Unfortunately, the very thing that the park was designed to protect—the petrified wood forests—continues to be in danger of disappearance. Every year, tons of petrified wood are stolen, often hidden in the pockets of otherwise honest visitors who believe "a little bit won't hurt." All visitors are asked to leave this great national resource intact so that future generations may also appreciate the wonders of the Petrified Forest.

PETROGLYPH NATIONAL MONUMENT

"Bear Shaman" petroglyph, Piedras Marcadas Unit.

"Lion" petroglyph, Rinconada Canyon.

The seventeen-mile-long dark shadow of the West Mesa escarpment that snakes alongside the Rio Grande in Albuquerque, New Mexico, is the focus of Petroglyph National Monument. This easy-to-reach monument was established in June 1990 to protect one of the most impressive collections of Indian and Hispanic rock art in the world. In addition, more than 100 archeological sites and a variety of volcanic features and associated wildlife habitats are protected, all within the Albuquerque city limits.

Human activity in the area goes back 12,000 years, but most of the rock art, consisting of approximately 17,000 petroglyphs incised on the West Mesa lava escarpment, was created by Pueblo Indians between A.D. 1300 and 1650—a period when contact with Europeans marked the transition from prehistoric to historic times. Known as Rio Grande Style rock art, these petroglyphs are some of the most dramatic in the Southwest in terms of number, content, style of execution, and complexity. Many designs closely relate to the symbols employed by contemporary Pueblo Indians, who continue to use sites in the monument today. Included is the familiar humpbacked flute player known as Kokopelli, along with an array of reptiles, birds, insects, four-legged animals, anthropomorphs, geometric designs, and intriguing masked serpents and star beings. Researchers believe that many of these symbols might have been created for ceremonial purposes, and their location on these exposed rocks was intrinsically significant. Perhaps inspired by the petroglyphs, later Hispanic settlers also made their own marks on the rock, incising crosses and other symbols alongside the many native designs.

The early fourteenth century saw a dramatic population increase in the Rio Grande region, resulting in major cultural advances in the native population. The unexcavated Piedras Marcadas pueblo site on the northeast side of the monument, with more than a thousand rooms on the ground floor alone, was one of many large pueblos, or villages, built to serve the growing population. At the base of the escarpment, the remains of field houses and water control features made of basalt indicate that some crop cultivation may have taken place beside the mesa, as well as along the fertile Rio Grande floodplain. These seasonal crops were supplemented with ricegrass and many other wild foods that grew along the mesa top, and with small game like deer and rabbits that inhabit the zone between the mesa and the floodplain.

During the early 1600s, pueblo populations in the area declined significantly due to migration and disease. These factors, together with economic exploitation by Spanish rule that exhausted resources, led to the Pueblo Revolt of 1680. The region was little inhabited until, following the Reconquest of 1692, Spanish cattle ranchers began to settle along the Rio Grande, and the pueblos of Isleta and Sandia were reoccupied by descendants of previous residents. Unable to resist, these ranchers also added their own still-visible inscriptions to the historical record preserved on the rocks' dark surfaces.

The monument's three units—Boca Negra, Piedras Marcadas, and Rinconada Canyon—are managed jointly by the National Park Service, the State of New Mexico, and the City of Albuquerque. The National Park Service is gradually implementing interpretive programs on the human history, wildlife, and geology of the monument.

VISITOR INFORMATION

Approximately 11 sq. mi. Parking fee at Boca Negra Unit. Monument is spread over the northwest section of town. Las Imagines Visitor Center open 8 A.M. to 5 P.M.: information, exhibits, and bookstore. From I-40 take Unser Blvd. north 3 miles to park visitor center; 5 miles to Boca Negra Unit. Information booth at Boca Negra. Hiking, picnicking, and nature watching at Boca Negra is encouraged; no picnicking is allowed at Piedras Marcadas. Allow 1 hour for petroglyphs at Boca Negra; 2 to 3 hours for Rinconada Canyon. Small parking lot at Rinconada. Scheduled ranger-led walks during summer months. Hot summers, with periods of rain from July through September. Winter days can be cold. The former Volcano Park contains 5 cinder cones, several geologic "windows," lava tubes, and other lava forms. Take Paseo del Volcan exit, north from I-40. Land is being added gradually to the monument. No camping in the monument. Visitor services (including campgrounds) available in Albuquerque. For more information, write: Superintendent, Petroglyph National Monument, 6001 Unser Blvd. NW, Albuquerque, NM 87120; or telephone (505) 899-0205. www.nps.gov/petr

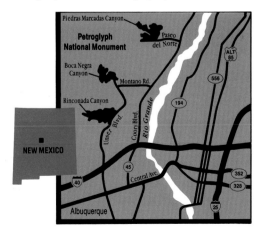

PIPE SPRING
NATIONAL MONUMENT

The parlor at
Winsor Castle.

VISITOR INFORMATION

40 acres. Entrance fee. Open year-round. Visitor center open 8 A.M. to 5 P.M.; call to check seasonal hours. Guided and self-guided tours, exhibits, gift store. Small adjoining campground run by Paiute Tribe. No lodging or gas, but cafeteria serving authentic cowboy fare on site. Nearest full facilities in St. George, Utah, on I-15, 85 miles away. For more information, write: Superintendent, Pipe Spring National Monument, HC 65-Box 5, Fredonia, AZ 86022; or telephone (520) 643-7105. www.nps.gov/pisp

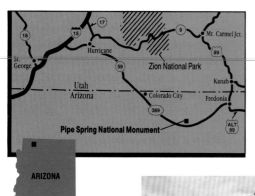

Winsor Castle.

Over the centuries, nomadic Indians, Mormon settlers, cattle ranchers, and thirsty travelers have relied on the water source at Pipe Spring in northern Arizona. The spring rises along the Sevier Fault on Hurricane Ridge, and its steady flow has earned Pipe Spring an important place in the history of the Arizona Strip.

Late nineteenth-century ranch buildings at Pipe Spring serve as reminders to today's comfortable travelers that courage, adventurousness, and self-sufficiency have been vital to human survival in this inhospitable desert. No one understood this better than the Anasazi Indians. They established a trading route through what is now the Arizona Strip to barter their corn, pinyon nuts, turquoise, and handicrafts with other native peoples. Eventually, they were superseded by hunter-gatherer Kaibab Paiutes. Traditional Paiutes were nomadic, living out of temporary brush shelters called *wickiups* and producing fine basketry, used for collecting and cooking wild crops and even as headgear. Modern-day Paiutes now live on a small reservation surrounding Spring.

In 1776, Fathers Silvestre Vélez de Escalante and Francisco Domínguez were the first white men to travel through the area, although they bypassed Pipe Spring by several miles. Eighty-two years later, Mormon missionary Jacob Hamblin, en route to Arizona's Hopi Mesas, was the first white to discover Pipe Spring. From then on, the spring was used by Mormon travelers heeding Brigham Young's call to Utah.

Dr. James Whitmore, a Texas cattle rancher, acquired Pipe Spring in 1863. He built a primitive dugout and fences and planted grape vines and, along with a herder named McIntyre, developed a ranching operation. The venture ended abruptly in 1866, when the two men were killed by Navajo raiders who had driven off some of their stock.

Major John Wesley Powell, the famous Western explorer and head of the U.S. Geologic Survey, visited Pipe Spring several times, living in one of the cabins on the grounds. In 1870, he and Jacob Hamblin, both renowned for their sensitivity in handling Indian affairs, negotiated a peace settlement between the Mormons and Navajos. The year before, Powell had charted the area surrounding the Colorado River and discovered that Pipe Spring was, in fact, in Arizona, not in Utah.

Undaunted by Indian raids and federal opposition to church mores, Brigham Young quickly appreciated Pipe Spring's strategic location for the tithing herd, the cattle contributed by Mormon families as a tenth of their incomes. In 1870, Anson Winsor and his wife Emeline were instructed to oversee contruction of a fortress to protect the valuable water supply, grazing grounds, and workers.

Winsor Castle, as it was called, consisted of two rectangular, two-story houses with walls connected at the end to form a courtyard. The fort and its outlying cabins, corral, pens, and ponds have been preserved very much as they were in their heyday. Cheese, butter, and beef were produced here and sent to St. George to sustain workers building the new Mormon temple. By 1879, the ranch supported more than 2,000 head of cattle.

After reaching its peak in the 1870s, the ranch was mainly used by Mormon newlyweds returning home following marriage ceremonies at the temple in St. George. Pipe Spring was sold to B. F. Saunders, a non-Mormon, in 1888. Saunders continued the cattle operation, serving the hungry markets back east. The ranch was eventually sold to Jonathon Heaton and his sons in 1906. Finding grazing lands depleted, the Heatons negotiated the final sale of Pipe Spring to the National Park Service in 1923. Today, it continues to serve as a reminder of the importance of ranching in early Western settlement and frontier living.

RAINBOW BRIDGE
NATIONAL MONUMENT

In 1908, the rock spans at Natural Bridges National Monument were studied and concluded to be the three finest and biggest natural bridges in the world. One year later, William Douglass, the surveyor who reached this conclusion, ate his words. Led by explorer John Wetherill and Indian guides Nasja Begay and Jim Mike, Douglass and archeologist Byron Cummings became the first whites to report the existence of an even larger and more spectacular natural bridge, just west of the previous three. It was dubbed Rainbow Bridge, after a Navajo legend, and, at a span of 275 feet, it remains the largest known natural bridge on earth.

Carved by Bridge Creek, which rises on Navajo Mountain and joins the Colorado River to the west, Rainbow Bridge is the stunning result of stream erosion of sedimentary rock. After millions of years of domination by seas, streams, tidal flats, and desert sand dunes, much of the Southwest lay covered by thousands of feet of sediments. Over time these sandwiched layers became rocks of alternating thicknesses and hardnesses, subject to movement according to the whim of ancient, underlying faults. One of the greatest of these movements began about 65 million years ago, eventually resulting in a mile-high uplift—the Colorado Plateau. Standing in relief, the plateau became vulnerable to water, wind, and temperature, all of which had a visible effect on newly exposed rock. Previously lackadaisical, wandering streams gathered force and downcut their paths. Here at Rainbow Bridge the scouring action of young Bridge Creek carved a meandering canyon, mainly consisting of pale pink, dune-formed Navajo Sandstone of the Jurassic Period supported by harder terra-cotta–colored Kayenta Sandstone.

Once entrenched in the canyon, the creek continued to carve its way through soft rock, but was forced to widen its path as it met resistant Kayenta Sandstone, thereby undercutting the canyon walls. Eventually, prodigious floodwater and debris ate through the meanders, resulting in an opening that allowed water to rush through. In this manner was Rainbow Bridge born, and, like all natural bridges, it will eventually collapse from its own weight and persistent wearing by wind and water.

The Navajo consider the site sacred; indeed, the vibrantly colored bridge does seem to be a portal admitting entrance to a secret world. In addition to being nature's sculptor, water has also invited many living things into this special place. Hanging gardens of fern and bright monkeyflower cling to seeping rocks, while on drier canyon walls, yucca, sego lily, aster, and evening primrose sustain themselves in pockets of soil. Sizzling

Rainbow Bridge.

summer temperatures ensure that the only animals you are likely to see in the daytime are sunbathing lizards and the occasional snake. Or your ears may pick up the sweet song of the canyon wren interrupting the eerie cawing of ravens that incessantly wheel overhead. But twilight attracts mule deer to the creek, bats reawaken, and coyotes "sing for their supper" while hunting mice. Harsh desert temperatures foster nocturnal habits, and to best learn about wildlife here it is advisable to follow nature's lead.

Until the creation of Lake Powell, Rainbow Bridge was accessible only to those hardy folk willing to hike the fourteen miles across rugged Navajo Reservation land to view it. This option is still popular, but now most people come by boat to marvel at this wonder of the world.

VISITOR INFORMATION

160 acres. Open year-round, all seasons recommended. No facilities or campgrounds in this remote monument, but these are available in surrounding Glen Canyon National Recreation Area reached by boat on Lake Powell. Visitors to the monument must either come by boat (Dangling Rope Marina lies close by, and there is a courtesy dock at the monument), or hike one of two trails overland from either Navajo Mountain Trading Post or the ruins of Rainbow Lodge, after obtaining permission from the Navajo Nation, Recreational Resources Dept., Box 308, Window Rock, AZ 86515. Information, interpretive exhibits, and bookstore available in the Carl Hayden Visitor Center at Glen Canyon National Recreation Area near Page, Arizona. For more information, write: Superintendent, Rainbow Bridge National Monument, P.O. Box 1507, Page, AZ 86040; or telephone (520) 608-6404. www.nps.gov/rabr

SAGUARO NATIONAL PARK

Saguaro cactus in bloom.

VISITOR INFORMATION

130.6 sq. mi. Park has 2 separate units on either side of Tucson. Full services are available in nearby Tucson. Summers are very hot and often wet; best time to visit is usually between March and May, when temperatures are most pleasant.

SAGUARO WEST (Tucson Mountain Unit) is open 24 hours year-round. Exhibits, information, bookstore, and interpretive activities at Red Hills Information Center, open 8:30 A.M. to 5 P.M. See this unit by taking 6-mile Bajada Loop Drive, short hikes such as Cactus Garden Trail, Discovery Nature Trail, and Valley View Overlook Trail, or longer hikes along intersecting trails. Horseback riding allowed on designated trails. No camping, but picnicking is available at one of 4 picnic areas. Nearest camping in the adjacent Tucson Mountain County Park. Nearby Arizona-Sonora Desert Museum provides an excellent introduction to Sonoran Desert natural history through living exhibits.

SAGUARO EAST (Rincon Mountain Unit) is open daily; call for hours. Visitor center open 8:30 A.M. to 5 P.M.: audiovisual program, exhibits, information, interpretive activities, bookstore. 8-mile Cactus Forest Drive winds through old-growth saguaro forest. Several short hikes begin along scenic drive. Longer hikes into the Rincon Mountains traverse several life zones along intersecting trails. Horseback riding allowed on designated trails. Backcountry camping available at designated sites with permit. 2 picnic areas. Adjoining Coronado National Forest has campgrounds, trails, and picnic areas. For more information, write: Superintendent, Saguaro National Park, 3693 South Old Spanish Trail, Tucson, AZ 85730-5601; or telephone (520) 733-5158 (Saguaro West), (520) 733-5153 (Saguaro East). www.nps.gov/sagu

By virtue of size, age, and unique adaptation to a harsh environment, the giant saguaro cactus is the undisputed king of Arizona's vast Sonoran Desert. As if to advertise the fact, ranks of saguaro march tirelessly across the desert, Shivalike "arms" frozen in a skyward salute — a powerful presence in an inscrutable landscape. Yet this plant, with its anthropomorphic postures, is but one of a fantastic array of interdependent life forms that make the Sonoran Desert the richest in variety in the world. In 1933, to protect and learn more about the saguaro, land containing a mature saguaro cactus forest was set aside east of Tucson as Saguaro National Park. A second unit west of the city, supporting younger saguaro growth, was added in 1961. This section is allowing more complete study of the lifespan of the saguaro.

Saguaros grow best on *bajadas*, or slopes of rock washed down from desert mountains. They may live up to 150 years, reach fifty feet in height, and weigh several tons. In a land of minimal rainfall, the saguaro's vast root network sucks up available moisture into a barrel-like torso supported by woody ribs. In a single rainstorm, the surface of a saguaro expands like an accordion to store up to 200 gallons of water in slow-to-evaporate gelatinous tissues — enough to last a whole year. Spines have replaced leaves and keep animals from the plant's precious water supply, trap cool air, provide shade, and, along with a waxy epidermis, protect the cactus from drying winds. In the absence of leaves, photosynthesis takes place in the saguaro's vast trunk and branching arms.

Although more than fifty kinds of cactus grow in the Sonoran Desert, the saguaro is particularly vital to the survival of other desert creatures. Birds like the gilded flicker and Gila woodpecker dig out nests in saguaro trunks where they keep cool and raise their young. Abandoned holes later attract screech owls, elf owls, cactus wrens, and other opportunists, while red-tailed and Harris hawks prefer to nest in the saguaro's upstretched arms. In late spring, stately saguaros grow a topknot of white blooms on the trunk and arms whose nectar provides food for Mexican white-winged doves and threatened long-nosed bats. Thus the cactus is pollinated, ensuring seeds for reproduction and tasty fruits for desert dwellers.

The eastern Rincon Mountain Unit highlights a forest of aging saguaro giants that can be visited by a drive on the eight-mile Cactus Forest Drive, or a hike through the forest. Backcountry trails into the Rincon Mountains reveal the varied geography of this section. With an elevation change from 2,600 to 8,666 feet, and an accompanying thirty-degree temperature drop and increased rainfall, the creosote bush, mesquite, and cacti of the desert gradually give way to grasslands, deciduous forests, and dense evergreen stands at mountain top. In cooler climes, desert survivalists like the kangaroo rat and the desert tortoise are replaced by peripatetic coyotes, shy bobcats, and high-flying hawks searching out small rodents. Canyons here hold evidence that Archaic hunter-gatherers and later Hohokam and Papago farmers relied on the streams and caves, gathered and prepared wild foods, and made tools from hard rock.

The turbulent geology of the entire Tucson Basin is particularly evident in the Tucson Mountain Unit, twenty-five miles west of Tucson. The jumbled rocks here are the result of millennia of volcanism, uplift, sedimentation, and erosion. On the flanks of the craggy Tucson Mountains, "nurse" trees, such as palo verde and ocotillo, shelter struggling saguaro seedlings, and throngs of youthful saguaro form dense stands. At the Signal Hill Picnic Area, petroglyphs incised in dark rocks are graphic reminders of the area's importance to generations of Sonoran Desert dwellers. Tohono O'odham Indians, like their ancestors the Hohokam and early Papago, still harvest saguaro fruit here to make jam, syrup, and ceremonial wine. Sunrise and sunset are particularly striking in this section of the monument, with its long vistas. At this time of day, the desert teems with activity as creatures emerge from cool burrows and begin the evening hunt.

The desert here seems unconquerable, yet the fragile balance can be easily disturbed by outside intrusion. Beginning in the late 1800s overgrazing of grasslands, mining for copper, and large-scale clearing of land for homes destroyed the habitat of many desert plants and animals. Subsequent erosion and flooding killed native species and allowed scrub to take over. Designation of the monument and elimination of grazing have allowed the desert to heal, but late twentieth-century urbanization is again threatening the wilderness. Its future lies in our hands.

SALINAS PUEBLO MISSIONS NATIONAL MONUMENT

The church at Quarai.

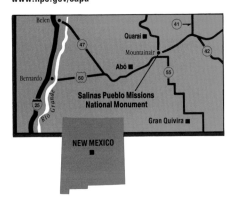

Salinas Pueblo Missions National Monument in central New Mexico preserves three of the oldest, most intact seventeenth-century Spanish missions in the United States. Gran Quivira received federal protection in 1909; the former state monuments of Abó and Quarai were added to form the new Salinas monument in 1980.

This is one of the best places in the Southwest to understand the epic struggle for survival and cultural dominance between seventeenth-century Spanish colonists and the native Pueblo people. Although these ruined pueblo missions appear similar at first glance, as you study the Pueblo and Spanish architecture and learn about the political upheavals and natural disasters that shook Spanish New Mexico, you will soon realize that Abó, Quarai, and Gran Quivira each has its own special story to tell.

The local limestone used to build Gran Quivira originated in a shallow sea that covered the area millions of years ago. As the climate became drier a large lake replaced the sea, which eventually evaporated, leaving behind the *salinas*, or salt beds, that were prized by later settlers. The first humans here were Paleo-Indian hunters who chased big game to the lakeshore. These nomads supplemented their meat-based diet with a variety of wild foods and slowly began to settle permanently in the area. By the tenth century, groups of residents, perhaps part of the Mogollon culture, were living here. Families lived in semisubterranean pit houses and used runoff from the mountains to irrigate small fields of corn, squash,

and beans, while continuing to hunt and gather like their predecessors. Farther south, near Gran Quivira, other groups used cisterns known as *pozos* to support a similar existence in the more arid land. By the 1100s, aboveground *jacal* structures made of brush chinked with mud were in vogue, perhaps as a result of Anasazi influences. Eventually, family groups joined other clans and began to build circular, then rectangular, apartment-style structures several stories high.

Abó, Quarai, and Gran Quivira were the sites of thriving villages known as pueblos. Strategically placed Gran Quivira became the southernmost trading hub between the Rio Grande pueblos and the Plains Apaches, as well as Mesoamerican and Pacific Coast Indians. Here was a bustling melting pot of native cultures who bartered animal products, pottery, feathers, pinyon nuts, corn, cloth, and more.

Change came for the pueblos with the colonizing efforts of the Spanish in 1598, which gathered force with the arrival of Franciscan missionaries bent on converting the Puebloans to Catholicism and the Spanish way of life. In 1622, Abó became the first to be missionized, under the guidance of Father Francisco Fonte. Quarai followed in 1626, under Father Juan Gutierrez de la Chica, and Father Francisco Letrado moved into Gran Quivira, or Las Humanas, as it was known, three years later. All three friars followed the usual procedures: arriving with start-up supplies and animals, they negotiated rooms in the pueblo from the *cacique*, or leader. If accepted, the friars

converted their rooms into living quarters, known as a *convento*, and a temporary chapel. Evidence of the first such chapel was found during the 1960s excavation of Mound 7 at Gran Quivira.

Construction of a larger church and convento began immediately. To make the missions completely self-supporting, the friars taught the Indians European methods of farming, construction, and other crafts. Abó exemplifies a typical mission, with its church, cemetery, *porteria* (waiting room), patio, *ambulatario* (walkway), cells, kitchens, storage rooms, and corrals. Abó also included the satellite parishes, or *visitas*, of Tenabo, Tabira, and Gran Quivira. As a mark of its importance, the small church of San Gregorio de Abó was replaced by a larger church in 1651. Like Quarai, it is a superb example of wall-and-lintel construction, with soaring walls, a nave, transepts, baptistry, choir loft, and a clerestory window.

Las Humanas pueblo and church at Gran Quivira.

Tabira black-on-white pottery canteen.

Doorway to baptistry at Abó.

The church and convento at Abó.

At Gran Quivira, lack of water forestalled missionary efforts. Father Francisco Letrado began the first church of San Isidro, but when he transferred to Zuni, Gran Quivira reverted to a visita of Abó. In 1659, resurgent royal support for the missions brought Father Diego de Santander to Gran Quivira. Santander began a new church, San Buenaventura, but never finished it. During the 1660s, here, as at other missions, resentment of Spanish rule and suppression of Indian beliefs was rife. The Spanish system of *encomienda*, which allowed favored Spanish colonists to collect grain and cloth from the Indians in return for military support, pitted government against Franciscan. Inquiries by the Spanish Inquisition, whose representatives sometimes quartered at Quarai, further factionalized friars, officials, and *encomenderos*.

Other pressures weakened the pueblos. Severe drought, mounting famine, and disease, which wiped out 450 people at Gran Quivira in 1668, together with attacks by former Apache trading partners, eventually forced the pueblos to dissolve. By the time the Pueblo Revolt erupted in 1680, the Salinas missions were empty, their inhabitants dispersed among the pueblos of the middle Rio Grande.

SUNSET CRATER VOLCANO NATIONAL MONUMENT

Sunset Crater Volcano from Bonito Park.

Aspen leaves on volcanic cinders.

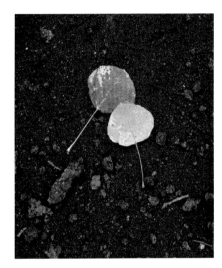

VISITOR INFORMATION

4.5 sq. mi. Entrance fee. Open year-round. Visitor center open 8 A.M. to 5 P.M. (to 6 P.M. in summer): exhibits, interpretive activities (mid-June through late August), information, bookstore. 36-mile loop road with pullouts and overlooks through Sunset Crater Volcano and Wupatki national monuments. Short Lava Flow Trail at the base of Sunset Crater highlights geology. The 44-site Bonito Campground is across from the visitor center; open between May 15 and Sept. 15 only and operated by U.S. Forest Service on a first-come, first-served basis; contact USFS, Peaks Ranger Station, 5075 N. Highway 89, Flagstaff, AZ 86004, tel. (520) 526-0866. Primitive camping in Cinder Hills Off-Road Vehicle Area on Forest Road 776. Nearest gas, food, and lodging in Flagstaff, 20 miles south. For more information, write: Superintendent, Sunset Crater Volcano National Monument, Rt. 3, Box 149, Flagstaff, AZ 86004; or telephone (520) 526-0502. www.nps.gov/sucr

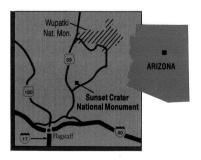

Sometime between 1064 and 1065, as William the Conqueror prepared to invade Britain, an eruption blasted through part of the large volcanic field east of the San Francisco Peaks in northern Arizona. This volcanic blast, which created Sunset Crater Volcano, was just one in a series of ongoing geologic events that helped shape the high-relief topography of this region.

To the west stand the towering San Francisco Peaks, formed by the collapse of the crater of a 15,000-foot ancestral volcano and subsequent ice age glaciation. The eleventh-century Sunset Crater eruption once more released molten lava from the earth, an event of simultaneous destruction and creation that built Sunset Crater Volcano's striking thousand-foot cinder cone and blanketed 800 square miles with ash and cinders. By the time the volcano ceased activity around 1250, it loomed over the desert, rimmed by fiery red cinders, with a 400-foot-deep crater at its center. Two large lava flows, the Bonito and Kana'a, stretched out on either side of Sunset Crater, while older sibling cinder cones, thrown up previously from the central vent, marched in perfect formation into the distance.

Sunset Crater Volcano's tumultuous landscape contrasts dramatically with the surrounding high desert plains and the colorful Painted Desert east of the monument. Little stirs here, except for the occasional Steller's jay, Abert squirrel, or raven. Despite the fertility of the volcanic soil, life has returned slowly. Stunted by aridity, scattered aspens and ponderosa pines cling precariously to the cindery soil. The lava flows seem like freshly plowed fields, their uneven, furrowed expanses the result of fast-cooling surface lava buckled by still-molten lava flowing below. This type of slow-moving lava is known by its Hawaiian name: *a'a*. The movement of molten lava through cooler material created lava tubes and caves, one of which is filled with ice year-round. Sentrylike geomorphs called squeezeups mark the escape routes of molten lava below. In places, cone-shaped vents known as fumaroles emitted sulfurous gases that left behind an artist's palette of colorful mineral deposits. Examples of these volcanic forms can be seen on the Lava Flow Nature Trail.

Four-and-a-half-square-mile Sunset Crater Volcano National Monument was designated in 1930 after strong local opposition to a plan by Hollywood filmmakers to blast the crater slopes during filming. In the sixties, NASA used the site as an astronaut training ground for the first moon landing. The area's Hopi and Navajo Indian inhabitants had several names for the rainbow-hued cone, but U.S. Geological Survey Director and famous explorer John Wesley Powell chose Sunset Peak (later renamed Sunset Crater) when he surveyed the area in 1885.

Sunset Crater Volcano's dramatic geological story is not the only feature of this monument. Bonito Park, near the entrance, contains evidence of early pit houses built by the Sinagua Indians, subsistence farmers who apparently fled before the eruption. Later generations returned to farm the fertile volcanic soil and, along with the Anasazi, developed a complex pueblo culture in the Wupatki Basin. Remains of this lifestyle may be viewed at Wupatki National Monument, an impressive group of Indian ruins eighteen miles northeast of Sunset Crater Volcano.

Living on the natural resources of the desert amid extreme temperatures is difficult to imagine. It is remarkable then that prehistoric people found a way to thrive in the Southwest, turning this dry desertscape into farmlands capable of feeding large populations. The Salado of the Tonto Basin in central Arizona were such a people. They farmed this remote area of the Sonoran Desert between A.D. 1150 and 1450. Tonto National Monument preserves and interprets two cliff dwellings built and occupied by the Salado during the fourteenth century.

The Salado, or "salt people," were named in the 1920s by archeologist Harold Gladwin for their home in Arizona's Salt River Valley. Their architecture and ceramics suggest that the Salado were a people of mixed cultural patterns influenced by neighboring Anasazi, Mogollon, and Hohokam. Around 1150, they built small, compact villages in the Tonto Basin, part of the Salt River Valley, planting crops of beans, amaranth, corn, cotton, and squash on the fertile bottomlands of the upper Salt River and on moist mountain slopes. A network of irrigation ditches ran from the river to their fields, but these have now been flooded by Roosevelt Lake. The Salado are renowned in the Southwest for their finely woven cotton garments and their superb polychrome pottery, featuring black-and-white-on-red designs.

Around 1300, groups of Salado moved to the high cliffs, most likely forced there by population growth in the valley below. They built several high-walled villages in natural limestone alcoves that offered shelter, a fine view, and access to useful natural resources like saguaro cacti, which thrive here on the slopes.

The lower village at Tonto National Monument, 350 feet above the valley, contained nineteen rooms and housed between forty and sixty people. Walls were built of rough quartzite, mortared crudely with mud. These were topped by mud-and-wood roofs, many of which can still be seen, as can the ghostly handprints of the workers in the mud. The small rooms of the pueblo were used mainly for sleeping and storage, and life was spent largely outside on the rooftops, which were surrounded by parapets.

The upper village, containing forty rooms, has evidently suffered the ravages of time. In the interests of preservation, visitors must now be accompanied by a park ranger when visiting the upper ruin. Although the view from the ruins now looks out onto Roosevelt Lake rather than a large desert basin, the essence of the place remains largely unchanged since Salado times.

Lower Ruin.

In little more than a century, these solidly constructed homes were abandoned by their occupants. The 1400s marked a general abandonment of the southern mountains of the Southwest. Why the Salado left and where they went has been hotly debated for many years. Several unproven theories have variously put forward that changing climatic patterns throughout the Southwest, crop failures due to salinization of overirrigated farmlands, and competition within the large population for shrinking natural resources may have caused their departure. Complex factors undoubtedly led to the Salado exodus from the Tonto Basin.

Even more intriguing is what became of the Salado. Some archeologists believe the emigrants moved north and west, joining the Zuni or Hopi pueblos and continuing their pueblo lifestyle; others hold that they went south to northern Mexico or into the lower Salt River Valley. When the first whites came to this area in the 1800s the only native occupants were Apache Indians; dubbed the Tonto by Spanish explorers, their name was given to this basin and its ruins.

VISITOR INFORMATION

1.75 sq. mi. Entrance fee. Open 8 A.M. to 5 P.M., except Christmas Day. Visitor center: audiovisual program, exhibits, information, bookstore. Self-guided tour of Lower Ruin (closes at 4 P.M.); ranger-led hike to Upper Ruin available in winter on a limited basis, by reservation only; hike is strenuous and requires 3 hours. Summers are hot, winters mild. No services in monument. Nearest facilities in Globe, 34 miles away. Surrounding Tonto National Forest offers plentiful hiking; boating, fishing, swimming, and picnicking at Roosevelt Lake; primitive camping beside Roosevelt and Apache lakes. For more information, write: Superintendent, Tonto National Monument, HC 02, Box 4602, Roosevelt, AZ 85545; or telephone (520) 467-2241. www.nps.gov/tont

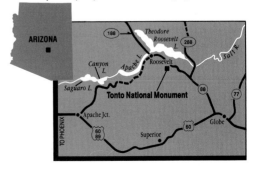

TUMACACORI
NATIONAL HISTORICAL PARK

The church at
Tumacácori.

The nave of the
church.

VISITOR INFORMATION

46 acres. Of the 3 missions, only Tumacácori is open to the public. Entrance fee. Open year-round 8 A.M. to 5 P.M. Visitor center. Museum has dioramas and other exhibits, information, bookstore. Historic craft demonstrations by Native Americans and Mexicans every weekend. Self-guiding trail through the garden and church. Desert vegetation blooms in early spring and late summer. Summers are fairly hot with occasional rainstorms; winters are mild. No camping in park, but picnicking is allowed. Nearest visitor services are in Tubac or the Mexican border town of Nogales. Park is within easy reach of Tucson, 47 miles north. For more information, write: Superintendent, Tumacácori National Historical Park, P.O. Box 67, Tumacácori, AZ 85640; or telephone (520) 398-2341. www.nps.gov/tuma

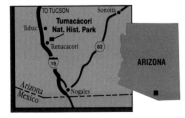

Tumacácori National Historical Park preserves the ruins of three churches built by Spanish colonists between the late 1600s and early 1800s in an effort to convert native people to Christianity. Upon their arrival, Spanish missionaries usually built a church and living quarters and quickly taught their converts European-style adobe construction, farming and ranching methods, and handicrafts. Self-sufficiency was important, not only for the welfare of the mission's inhabitants but also to maintain steady supply lines to other Spanish settlers, who were frequently allowed to benefit from mission wealth in return for settling new lands.

Pimería Alta, which included present-day southern Arizona, was Mexico's northernmost province and the traditional home of the Pima Indians. The first Spanish missionary to explore the area was Father Eusebio Francisco Kino, a German-educated, Italian Jesuit, who founded his first mission here in 1687 and continued to explore the region until his death in 1711. In 1691, at the request of the villagers, Father Kino brought Christianity to the settlement on the Santa Cruz River which he named San Cayetano de Tumacácori. In the same year, he also founded a mission site at Guevavi, a village to the southeast, and began traveling to both areas to say mass and to instruct the residents in growing wheat and raising cattle, goats, and sheep. In 1701, San Gabriel de Guevavi was designated the district headquarters, and a small church was built there. Tumacácori became a *visita*, or satellite parish, of Guevavi. It was visited regularly by Guevavi's new resident priest, Father Juan de San Martín, who conducted mass and oversaw mission activities. Construction of a new church began at Guevavi when Father

Garucho was assigned to the mission in 1751. In 1767, however, the Jesuits were recalled from the colonies, and this together with the earlier Pima Rebellion of 1756, Apache raiding, and disease, weakened the Guevavi mission. It was completely abandoned in 1771.

Tumacácori, which had been relocated to its present site following the Pima Revolt and renamed San José de Tumacácori, became district headquarters for the Franciscan missionaries sent to replace the Jesuits. The remaining mission in the area, San Cayetano de Calabazas, now came under its jurisdiction. Father Narciso Gutiérrez came to Tumacácori in 1794 and began to build a large new church. Construction began in 1800, but the new church was not in use until two years after Father Gutiérrez's death in 1820. Mexico won her independence from Spain in 1821, and most missions were abandoned as a result. Laws were passed that required remaining missions to become parish churches. At Tumacácori, Apache raids grew worse and went unopposed by the Mexican government. In 1848, residents gathered up their belongings and relocated to San Xavier del Bac in Tucson. The United States acquired the territory in June 1854, and ranchers moved into the area. They used the cemetery at Tumacácori as a corral, and the mission deteriorated for the rest of the century. Tumacácori became a national monument in 1908. It was redesignated a national historical park in August 1990, and the missions of Calabazas and Guevavi were added.

That the church at Tumacácori still stands is remarkable testimony to the skills of the Indian craftsmen who built it. High adobe walls frame a long nave running north to south, the domed sanctuary is still intact, as is a distinctive fired brick belltower. The *convento* adjoining the church on the east is typical of the period, containing a large central patio surrounded by living quarters for the priests, storerooms, workshops, classrooms, and granaries.

The fertile Verde Valley in central Arizona, a natural corridor between the state's southern desert and northern plateau, was a prehistoric crossroads. It became the home of both Sinagua and Hohokam cultures and was frequented by Mogollon and Anasazi traders from the east and north, respectively. Evidence of the resulting exchange of ideas may be seen today in the ruins of an eleventh- to fifteenth-century Sinagua pueblo preserved at Tuzigoot National Monument.

The Sinagua people here were originally dryland farmers, living in modest pit houses in the uplands and supplementing their diet with hunting and gathering. In the tenth century they shared the Verde Valley with the Hohokam, famed for their elaborate irrigation systems and for their ball games, played in walled ball courts. Following the eruption in 1065 of Sunset Crater Volcano, groups of Sinagua and Hohokam moved to the volcanic lava fields just northeast of modern-day Flagstaff, Arizona, to capitalize on newly fertile land and increased rainfall. The Sinagua who stayed behind took advantage of the vacated Hohokam areas in the Verde Valley bottomlands, moving in and adopting Hohokam irrigation methods. They cultivated corn, squash, beans, and cotton and built aboveground masonry buildings in the manner of the Anasazi. Mogollon neighbors taught the Sinagua how to fashion rough, red pots for cooking and storage. The Sinagua themselves were proficient at making stone implements and cotton clothing.

In A.D. 1000, several families moved onto a ridge and built a small, two-story, stone pueblo, later named Tuzigoot, or "crooked water," by Apaches, after the crescent-shaped lake nearby. During a long drought in the late 1200s, Sinagua people from the north moved into the valley, searching for reliable water sources. As a result, the population of Tuzigoot grew, and the pueblo expanded southward down the hill. In contrast to some drier regions, life here was comfortable, with plentiful antelope, deer, bear, and wildfowl for food and clothing, and the year-round Verde River to irrigate crops. Trade with neighboring cultures grew, and food, cotton, and possibly salt were bartered for prized turquoise, shells, and ceramics.

In the 1300s the pueblo grew even more, to 110 rooms, to house new arrivals. This expansion severely stressed natural resources and seems to have put pressure on valley residents. Storage of food became vital, and the appearance of the pueblo suggests possible fortification, although this has never been proved. Entrance to the village was now afforded by ladders to the rooftop and ceiling hatchways. Nevertheless, overcrowding, failing natural resources, and epidemics appar-

The restored ruins of Tuzigoot.

ently took their toll; by 1425 the Sinagua had moved away. Modern residents of Arizona's Hopi Mesas tell stories of ancestors in a fertile region to the south they call Palatkwapi, and people of Zuni Pueblo also trace ancestry to the Verde Valley; however, their claims, apparently supported by numerous instances of identical ceremonial practices and artwork, remain unproved.

Spaniard Antonio de Espejo was the first white man to see Tuzigoot, in 1583, but until railroad surveyors mapped the territory in the mid-1800s, little attention was paid to the prehistoric ruins. The end of that century saw archeologists assessing the site, but incessant pothunting threatened research. Then-University of Arizona professor Byron Cummings and his students excavated the site in the 1920s, trenching and charting. Two students of Cummings's, Louis Caywood and Edward Spicer, undertook a Works Project Administration (WPA) survey of the ruins between 1934 and 1935 and conducted the first full-scale excavation of Tuzigoot. Previously owned by the United Verde Copper Company, the site had been deeded to the Verde School District. In 1939, the school district officially turned over the ruins and their artifacts to the National Park Service, whereupon Tuzigoot received full protection as a national monument.

VISITOR INFORMATION

43 acres. Entrance fee. Open year-round 8 A.M. to 5 P.M. (to 7 P.M. in summer). Visitor center: exhibits, interpretive activities, information, bookstore. Self-guided trail through ruins. No facilities at monument; these may be found in Clarkdale, Cottonwood, and throughout the Verde Valley. Surrounding area is scenic, with plentiful hiking, backpacking, and camping in national forest. National forest campgrounds often fill in summer. Advance reservations are recommended; call 1-877-444-6777. Camping also at Dead Horse Ranch State Park, (520) 634-5283. A visit to nearby Montezuma Castle is recommended. For more information, write: Superintendent, Tuzigoot National Monument, P.O. Box 68, Clarkdale, AZ 86324; or telephone (520) 634-5564. www.nps.gov/tuzi

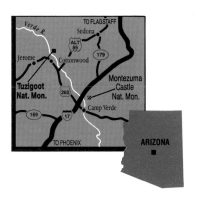

WALNUT CANYON NATIONAL MONUMENT

Remains of a cliff dwelling.

VISITOR INFORMATION

5.5 sq. mi. Entrance fee. Open year-round 9 A.M. to 5 P.M. (8 A.M. to 6 P.M. between Memorial Day and Labor Day); closed Christmas. Visitor center: audiovisual and interpretive programs, exhibits, information, bookstore. A steep ³/₄-mile trail leads through ruins, and a ¹/₂-mile rim trail provides overlook views of the canyon ruins; two ruins near mesa-top fields may be glimpsed from this point. Picnicking permitted in monument (no fires or charcoal allowed). No services; nearest facilities are in Flagstaff, 7.5 miles away. For more information, write: Superintendent, Walnut Canyon National Monument, Walnut Canyon Road #3, Flagstaff, AZ 86004; or telephone (520) 526-3367. www.nps.gov/waca

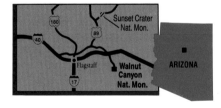

Sinagua redware bowl.

The cliff dwellings in Walnut Canyon National Monument in northern Arizona are so well preserved you almost forget that they have been empty since A.D. 1250. Today, it is still easy to see what attracted early humans to live in the canyon: sheltering rock overhangs with warm southern exposures, relatively reliable water, plant and animal life, and mesa tops that could be cleared for fields. For the Sinagua people, accustomed to dryland living (their Spanish name means "without water"), this was a bountiful place.

Early Sinaguans built occasional pit houses here around the tenth century. Then, in 1125, following eruptions that created nearby Sunset Crater, a new generation of Sinagua farmers in search of fertile lands began to utilize the canyon. They built small houses directly under limestone overhangs in the cliffs, 150 feet above the canyon bottom. They grew corn, squash, and beans on the mesa tops, using a network of paths to reach their fields and gain access to water. With no need to build roofs, Sinagua masons concentrated on mud-mortaring rocks into a facade beneath the overhangs and fashioned T-shaped doors for ventilation and access. Nearly 300 small, plastered rooms are strung along the cliffs. Their snug size indicates they were used mainly for sleeping, cooking, and storage; all other activities took place outdoors.

Five islandlike "forts" were also built on rocky promontories around Walnut Canyon. Although these buildings appear defensive, no evidence of warfare has been found. The Sinagua were apparently a highly organized people, with strong religious traditions, causing some researchers to suggest that leaders used the forts, and that ceremonial gatherings took place in them. Field houses on the rims allowed residents to watch their crops during the short growing season at this 7,000-foot elevation. To supplement their diet and to provide clothing, the Sinagua hunted deer, bighorn sheep, rabbits, and other small game, and kept wild turkeys. Wild foods like pinyon nuts and tubers also played a vital role.

Mesa-top fields were watered solely by rainfall, at best an unreliable quantity in the Southwest. Check dams, which held back small pockets of soil, helped maximize use of rainwater. Some archeologists believe the Sinagua learned building and water conservation techniques from earlier contact with neighboring Anasazi people. Trade among the peoples of the Southwest was apparently very important. The Sinagua may have exchanged food and perhaps their distinctive pottery for precious stones and shells, which they made into elaborate jewelry, and for cotton cloth, which was used to make clothing.

After just 125 years here, the Sinagua began to drift away. Various environmental factors, many common throughout the Southwest, may have contributed: a long drought in the 1200s, a break-down in trade, or perhaps depletion of resources due to overpopulation. Cultural similarities strongly suggest that some of their number moved to the Hopi Mesas; many Hopis consider Sinagua sites ancestral homes. Ritual burials have been uncovered in Sinagua territory that have contained ceremonial artifacts, such as finely carved wands and ornate jewelry, still employed in contemporary Hopi ceremonies. We owe much of our present understanding of the Sinagua culture to the work of Dr. Harold Colton, who surveyed Walnut Canyon in the 1930s.

In 1883, the transcontinental railroad began to promote sightseeing to Walnut Canyon. The resulting popularity almost destroyed the ruins until establishment of the national monument in 1915. Eighteen years later, Walnut Canyon got its first full-time National Park Service ranger, who worked closely with the newly formed Civilian Conservation Corps to expand and improve the monument facilities and to protect the ruins.

WHITE SANDS NATIONAL MONUMENT

The snow white dunes of White Sands National Monument, undulating across southern New Mexico's vast Tularosa Basin, make up the largest gypsum desert in the world, and perhaps the most alien landscape in the Southwest. But the origins of this strange sight are quite earthly, and close by. The dunes are a direct result of gypsum washed down into the basin from the San Andres Mountains to the west and the Sacramento Mountains to the east.

On reaching the Tularosa Basin, alkaline gypsum sediments accumulate in intermittent Lake Lucero and other small lakes, where they join existing gypsum deposits in groundwater pulled to the surface by capillary action. The sizzling temperatures of the Chihuahuan Desert soon evaporate the water, leaving daggerlike gypsum crystals, which are then blasted apart by extreme temperatures and southwesterly winds that sweep across the valley in springtime. The fine, white gypsum grains are scooped up and blown northeastward toward the facing Sacramento Mountains. Strong winds cause sand-sized grains to bounce along the ground, where they form dunes of different shapes and sizes that, in turn, affect further deposition. Despite apparent immobility, the form of the dunes changes ceaselessly.

These mountains are gypsum-rich because of a fascinating past. Salt and gypsum evaporated from a landlocked sea here 250 million years ago. Sixty-five million years later, sediments were arched upward, then began to settle along deep fault lines. Finally, around 10 million years ago, movement along faults caused the domed crust to sink and form a deep basin. Thus, the San Andres and Sacramento mountains are the two ends of a collapsed dome, separated by the Tularosa Basin.

White Sands National Monument was created in 1933 to protect and interpret this unique environment. Different types of dunes and the plants that have gained a foothold in their shifting

Dunes and San Andres Mountains.

Yucca in dune.

mass are found here. The periphery contains parabolic dunes that have been stabilized by vegetation and mineral crystalization beneath the surface. Here grow yucca, four-wing saltbush, iodinebush, and other plants that can tolerate the alkaline habitat. Western diamondback and desert massasauga rattlesnakes lie motionless in their shade, while kangaroo rats burrow beneath the dunes to keep cool. In these brilliant white surroundings, almost anything stands out, so some dune creatures, such as mice and lizards, adopt a white camouflage to avoid this. Desert animals are generally nocturnal, preferring cooler evening temperatures. Kit foxes, coyotes, and other rodent hunters animate the desert as the sun goes down. Birds of many kinds make their home along the dune margins. Finches, doves, thrashers, and shrikes give up the skies at night to nighthawks and owls. The Big Dune Trail loop offers a pleasant, short hike through this environment.

Near the center of the monument, crescent-shaped barchan dunes and long ridges of transverse dunes form where sand is most plentiful. Some dunes reach sixty feet high here. They migrate northeastward as much as twelve feet a year. Picnicking at the picnic area in the midst of these giants is an unforgettable experience. Low dome-shaped frontier dunes are found far to the southwest corner of the monument near Lake Lucero, where winds are strongest. The fast-moving sand allows few plants to grow here. Due to its proximity to White Sands Missile Range (site of the first atomic bomb test in 1945), this area of the monument may only be visited once a month as part of a ranger-led tour.

VISITOR INFORMATION

228 sq. mi. Entrance fee. Open year-round. Visitor center open 7 A.M. to 4:30 P.M. (winter), 7 A.M. to 9 P.M. (summer): audiovisual program, exhibits, information, bookstore, and gift shop. 16-mile Dunes Drive loop open 7 A.M. to 10 P.M. (summer), closing at sunset in winter. Self-guided nature trail and dune hike. Dunes open until midnight on full moon nights during summer. 3-hour, ranger-led tours of Lake Lucero available monthly by advance reservation. Backcountry hiking and camping in primitive backcountry campground with permit; nearest public campgrounds in Lincoln National Forest, 35 miles east, and at Aguirre Springs, 30 miles west. Picnicking. Full visitor services in Alamogordo. For more information, write: Superintendent, White Sands National Monument, P.O. Box 1086, Holloman AFB, NM 88330; or telephone (505) 479-6124. www.nps.gov/whsa

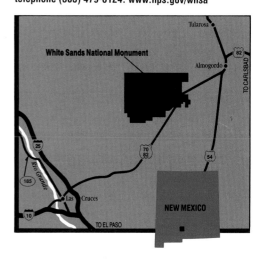

WUPATKI NATIONAL MONUMENT

Tall House Ruin.

Textile-pattern petroglyph.

VISITOR INFORMATION

55 sq. mi. Open year-round, although snow sometimes closes 18-mile approach road from Highway 89. Visitor center hours are 8 A.M. to 5 P.M. (to 6 P.M. in summer): exhibits, interpretive programs, information, bookstore. A 35.3-mile paved road with many fine vista points runs south from Highway 89 through Wupatki to Sunset Crater Volcano National Monument; distance is 18 miles between monuments. Self-guided trail through main Wupatki Ruins recommended. Nearest gas, food, and lodging are in Flagstaff, 50 miles south; Bonito Campground at Sunset Crater, containing 44 campsites, is operated in summer by U.S. Forest Service on a first-come, first-served basis. For more information, write: Superintendent, Wupatki National Monument, HC 33, Box 444A, Flagstaff, AZ 86004; or telephone (520) 679-2365. www.nps.gov/wupa

The exposed high country just east of the San Francisco Peaks in northern Arizona is exceptionally dry and supports only the occasional stunted juniper and adaptable desert creatures; it is an unlikely spot in which to build a community. Nevertheless, preserved at Wupatki National Monument are more than 2,000 Indian ruins, the remains of structures built between A.D. 500 and 1400.

Around A.D. 500, the eastern flanks of the San Francisco Peaks were home to a group of early farmers known as the Sinagua, meaning "without water" in Spanish. Paleo-hunters once roamed here, too, as evidenced by recent discovery of an 11,000-year-old Clovis spear point. Living in reinforced pit houses with small ceremonial chambers, or kivas, the Sinagua took advantage of runoff to irrigate corn crops, collected edible plants, and hunted small game living in the mixed life zones found from the mountains to the desert grasslands.

Then, around 1064, they fled during a series of terrifying volcanic eruptions that shook the region. Blankets of erupting ash and cinders buried the old Sinagua homesteads and, just to the south, Sunset Crater arose. The determined Sinagua did not abandon their ancestral homes for long, though. By the end of the eleventh century they were back farming the 5,000-foot elevations, attracted by increased rainfall and the moisture-retaining properties of ash-covered soil. Slowly, they rebuilt their homes and began to have contact with other Indian cultures moving about the area.

The Sinagua in the Wupatki Basin soon were joined by the Cohonina from the west and the Kayenta Anasazi from the northeast, all apparently lived in harmony on the land, sharing knowledge and beliefs, and possibly even intermarrying. The adaptable Sinagua began to expand their range. From the Anasazi they learned how to build pueblos; the multileveled, masonry villages of Lomaki, the Citadel, Wukoki, and Wupatki itself are examples. Concentrations of small pueblos have been found on Antelope Prairie and the shallow volcanic valley next to the Citadel, indicating the Sinagua's willingness to locate wherever arable land was most plentiful. The Anasazi also taught the Sinagua how to build water catchment systems to maximize meager rainfall. New religious beliefs brought the community together in the enormous amphitheater close to Wupatki ruin.

The Cohonina contributed new ceramic methods, resulting in the development of beautiful, utilitarian pottery. One structure at the monument is thought to have been a ball court, as it bears a close structural resemblance to ball courts found in southern Arizona and in Mesoamerica. Its presence seems to indicate close trading ties with those areas. Although it is unclear what the Wupatki residents themselves traded, parrot and macaw feathers and copper from Mesoamerica were prized acquisitions, as were shells obtained from Pacific cultures.

Many petroglyphs at Wupatki seem to represent important leaders, and some researchers think that larger ruins like the Citadel and Wupatki were occupied by powerful members of the community. Other theories hold that the tall, beautifully constructed buildings here may also have been astronomic lookouts or perhaps boundary markers.

By the 1200s drought had set in. The people of Wupatki gradually began to move away until by 1400 no one remained. Shared beliefs, petroglyphs, and stories about ancestral homelands link today's Hopi culture to the Sinagua. Navajos, too, inhabited Wupatki from the 1820s until establishment of the national monument in 1924. Layer upon layer of human experience haunts this desolately beautiful environment, endowing it with a spiritual quality not quickly forgotten.

The West Temple and Towers of the Virgin.

VISITOR INFORMATION

229 sq. mi. Entrance fee. South and East entrances lead into the park. Note: large vehicles, such as motorhomes, trailers, and buses, must make an advance reservation at the entrance station and pay a fee to be escorted through Zion Tunnel. Escorts only available between 8 A.M. and 8 P.M. during the summer (shorter hours other seasons). Alternate routes are available. Both Zion Canyon and Kolob District units of the park and their visitor centers open year-round (call for seasonal hours); some other services spring through fall only. Both have audiovisual and interpretive programs and bookstores. Summers are often hot and over-crowded; off-season is recommended. Hikes of varying difficulty, scenic drives, and conces-sionaire-operated horseback and tram tours from Zion Lodge. 2 campgrounds operated on first-come, first-served basis. 374 campsites; a third campground open summer only, 6 sites, no water; group sites by reservation. Zion Lodge (open year-round), tel. (303) 297-2757. Nearest full visitor services in Springdale, Mt. Carmel Junction, St. George, Cedar City, and Kanab. For more infor-mation, write: Superintendent, Zion National Park, Springdale, UT 84767; or telephone (435) 772-3256. www.nps.gov/zion

These great mountains are natural temples of God. We can worship here as well as in the man-made temples in Zion, the biblical "Heavenly City of God." Let us call it Little Zion.

—Attributed to Isaac Behunin, early Mormon settler

Set amid the spectacular maze of southern Utah's colorful mesas, Zion Canyon's sheltered, 2,000-foot walls and dramatic Navajo Sandstone formations have attracted human interest for more than 1,500 years. Pre-Columbian Anasazi Indians, followed by Paiutes, who were later displaced by nineteenth-century Mormon immigrants, have all sought physical and spiritual sustenance in this bountiful canyon. Protected since 1919 as a national park, Zion continues to draw travelers with its extraordinary geological marvels and natural diversity.

Two hundred million years of changing environments—inland seas, lakes, streams, and tall sand dunes—are responsible for this rocky masterpiece. Thick beds of sands, silts, and limy animal skeletons were laid down and eventually coalesced into soft sedimentary sandstones. In Zion, eight such sandstone layers have been exposed, the most prominent of which is the Navajo Sandstone, which reaches 2,400 feet thick. This creamy pink rock is all that remains to tell us of a time when hot, dry winds blew sand into high dunes across the Southwest. About 13 million years ago, the southern Colorado Plateau rose up, break-ing and weathering along faults into distinctive tablelands. Water, ice, and snow then slowly sculpted the sandstone into deep, curving canyons decorated with alcoves, arches, and spires.

Zion Canyon itself is the work of the North Fork of the Virgin River. From its 9,000-foot source high on the Markagunt Plateau, the Virgin cuts a path through the sandstone to Lake Mead on the Colorado River. Zion Narrows, a slot canyon approximately 2,000 feet deep and only twenty feet wide in places, is a particularly impressive example of the Virgin River's erosional power. The sheer walls of the Narrows begin to widen only when they reach the softer Kayenta Sandstone, where the Navajo Formation has been undercut by erosion of the softer Kayenta rock below. Throughout Zion towering rock landmarks, such as the Temple of Sinawava, the Watchman, and the Great White Throne, reflect the region's dramatic geological history.

(continued)

Manzanita buds.

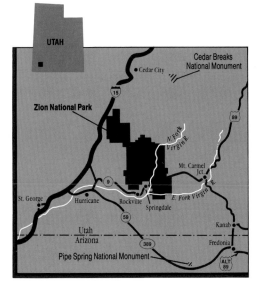

Sandstone cliffs, Kolob Canyon.

The Virgin River at the Narrows.

The park ranges in elevation from 3,666 feet to 8,726 feet and encompasses four major life zones. At the lower elevations juniper-pinyon forests prosper, interspersed with serviceberry, singleleaf ash, manzanita, cliff rose, and cacti. Patches of Gambel oak and scrub oak grow here, along with colorful bigtooth maple. Indian paintbrush and the purple flowers of chorispora dot the canyon floor in spring, along with sego lilies and violets. Sacred datura, also known as Zion lily, which blooms during cooler evening and morning temperatures, forms a delightful carpet of trumpet flowers in the summer. Dense stands of Fremont cottonwoods, box elders, velvet ash, and several kinds of willows flourish beside streams, along with exotic tamarisk, an unwelcome invader throughout the Southwest.

The higher, wetter elevations support ponderosa pine, Rocky Mountain juniper, and sagebrush, as well as Gambel oak, Douglas fir, white fir, and dazzling quaking aspen. Seeps and springs flow out where water descending through porous Navajo Sandstone meets the impervious Kayenta Sandstone. Here are unexpected "hanging gardens" of ferns, lichens, shooting stars, and monkeyflowers; the unique Zion snail is also found in such places. Gateway to the Narrows and Weeping Rock trails offer beautiful examples. Differing light and moisture conditions in the canyons also foster interesting blends of life zones.

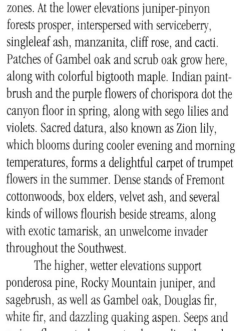

White Arch.

Prickly pear cactus.

The largest mammal seen at Zion is the mule deer. Deer form the main diet of the mountain lion, but you are unlikely to glimpse this secretive creature or another shy resident, the reintroduced bighorn sheep. Bobcat, coyote, gray fox, badger, and weasel live here, as do ringtail cats, notorious camp robbers. Antelope ground squirrels and rock squirrels, though charming, can also be a nuisance. Of special interest to river watchers are beavers, known locally as bank beavers, which make their home here. The largest lizard in Zion is the slow-moving chuckwalla, but also commonly found are whiptails and desert spiny lizards. Snakes are found at all elevations. The Western rattlesnake is occasionally seen.

More than a hundred birds breed here, including hummingbirds, golden eagles, and rare peregrine falcons. Of the sixty permanent residents, you are likely to see robins, black-headed grosbeaks, mountain and black-capped chickadees, American flickers, blue-gray gnatcatchers, and hairy woodpeckers. The distinctive falling register of the canyon wren delights hikers. But its sweet song may be drowned out by noisy ravens, pinyon jays, and Steller's jays.

Visitors arriving at the park from the East Entrance go through the impressive Zion–Mount Carmel Tunnel. Completed in 1930, this new highway avoided a hazardous stretch of mountain road through the Arizona Strip and shortened the distance to Bryce Canyon by seventy miles, and to the Grand Canyon by twenty miles. The scenic drive adjoining the tunnel makes an excellent introduction to Zion, but hiking along one of the more than a dozen trails is the best way to see the park.

Zion's broad acreage includes the narrow, 1,600-feet-deep Finger Canyons of the Kolob District in the north, reached by way of Interstate 15. The Kolob Canyons also contain Kolob Arch, a magnificent freestanding arch with a 310-foot span, perhaps one of the largest arches in the world.

The Great White Throne and The Organ.

Maple leaves in Refrigerator Canyon.

Court of the Patriarchs and the Virgin River.

Nuttall's cottontail.

ACKNOWLEDGMENTS

This book is more than just a park guide; it is a celebration of the many attributes that combine to make America the richly diverse country it is today. It was a privilege to work with the staffs of the national parks and cooperating associations whose dedication to the national park mission was inspiring. These numerous individuals spent many hours talking with us about their parks and reviewing written pieces. We thank them for their help. The author also wishes to acknowledge Jeff Book, for his support over the years, and Tim Goodwin, whose love and companionship have enriched her southwestern odyssey. The photographer thanks Christina Watkins, the book's designer, for her encouragement during this project, and for sharing her enthusiasm and love of these national parks.

SUGGESTED READING LIST

Abbey, Edward. *Desert Solitaire: A Season in the Wilderness*. [1968]. Reprint. Tucson: University of Arizona Press, 1988.

Crampton, C. Gregory. *Standing Up Country: The Canyon Lands of Utah and Arizona*. [1964]. Reprint. Salt Lake City: Peregrine Smith Books, 1983.

Fletcher, Colin. *The Man Who Walked Through Time*. [1968]. Reprint. New York: Random House, 1989.

Krutch, Joseph W. *The Desert Year*. [1952]. Reprint. Tucson: University of Arizona Press, 1990.

Lavender, David. *The Southwest*. [1980]. Reprint. Albuquerque: University of New Mexico Press, 1984.

Lister, Florence C., and Robert W. Lister. *Those Who Came Before: Southwestern Archeology in the National Park System*. Tucson: Southwest Parks and Monuments Association, 1983.

Lopez, Barry Holstun. *Desert Notes: Reflections in the Eye of a Raven*. [1979]. Reprint. New York: Avon Books, 1981.

Nabhan, Gary Paul. *Gathering the Desert*. Tucson: University of Arizona Press, 1985.

Schaafsma, Polly. *Indian Rock Art of the Southwest*. Santa Fe: School of American Research, 1980.

Stegner, Wallace. *Beyond the Hundredth Meridian: John Wesley Powell and the Second Opening of the West*. [1954]. Reprint. New York: Viking Penguin, 1992.

Van Dyke, John Charles. *The Desert*. [1918]. Reprint. Salt Lake City: Gibbs Smith Publisher, 1991.

Zwinger, Ann. *Wind in the Rock*. Tucson: University of Arizona Press, 1978.

ਬੌਨੇ ਅਤੇ ਮੋਚੀ

The Elves and the Shoemaker

retold by Henriette Barkow
illustrated by Jago

Panjabi translation by Kulwant Manku

mantra lingua

ਇੱਕ ਵਾਰੀ ਦੀ ਗੱਲ ਹੈ ਇੱਕ ਮੋਚੀ ਅਤੇ ਉਸਦੀ ਪਤਨੀ ਸੀ। ਮੋਚੀ ਬਹੁਤ ਮਿਹਨਤ ਨਾਲ ਕੰਮ ਕਰਦਾ ਸੀ ਪਰ ਫੈਸ਼ਨ ਬਦਲਣ ਕਰਕੇ ਲੋਕਾਂ ਨੇ ਉਸਤੋਂ ਜੁੱਤੀਆਂ ਖਰੀਦਣੀਆਂ ਬੰਦ ਕਰ ਦਿੱਤੀਆਂ। ਉਹ ਗਰੀਬ ਤੋਂ ਗਰੀਬ ਹੁੰਦਾ ਗਿਆ। ਅਖੀਰ ਵਿੱਚ ਉਸਦੇ ਕੋਲ ਸਿਰਫ ਇੱਕ ਜੋੜਾ ਜੁੱਤੀਆਂ ਬਣਾਉਣ ਦਾ ਹੀ ਚਮੜਾ ਰਹਿ ਗਿਆ।

Once there lived a shoemaker and his wife. He worked hard, but fashions changed and people didn't buy his shoes any more. He became poorer and poorer. In the end he only had enough leather to make one last pair of shoes.

ਕਤਰ, ਕਤਰ! ਉਸਨੇ ਇੱਕ ਜੋੜਾ ਜੁੱਤੀ ਬਣਾਉਣ ਲਈ ਚਮੜਾ ਕੱਟਿਆ।

Snip, snip! He cut out the shapes of two shoes.

ਉਸਨੇ ਤਿਆਰ ਕੀਤੇ ਚਮੜੇ ਨੂੰ ਸਵੇਰ ਨੂੰ ਸਿਉਣ ਵਾਸਤੇ ਕੰਮ ਕਰਨ ਦੇ ਅੱਡੇ ਤੇ ਰੱਖ ਦਿੱਤਾ।

He left them on the workbench ready to start sewing in the morning.

ਅਗਲੇ ਦਿਨ ਸਵੇਰੇ ਜਦੋਂ ਉਹ ਹੇਠਾਂ ਆਇਆ ਤਾਂ ਉਸਨੂੰ... ਇੱਕ ਬਹੁਤ ਸੋਹਣਾ ਜੁੱਤੀਆਂ ਦਾ ਜੋੜਾ ਮਿਲਿਆ। ਉਸਨੇ ਜੁੱਤੀਆਂ ਨੂੰ ਚੁੱਕਿਆ ਅਤੇ ਦੇਖਿਆ ਕਿ ਹਰੇਕ ਤੋਪਾ ਪ੍ਰਬੀਨਤਾ ਨਾਲ ਲੱਗਾ ਹੋਇਆ ਸੀ। "ਮੈਂ ਹੈਰਾਨ ਹਾਂ ਕਿ ਇਹ ਜੁੱਤੀਆਂ ਕਿਸਨੇ ਬਣਾਈਆਂ ਹਨ?" ਉਸਨੇ ਸੋਚਿਆ।

The next day, when he came downstairs, he found... a beautiful pair of shoes.
He picked them up and saw that every stitch was perfectly sewn.
"I wonder who made these shoes?" he thought.

ਉਸੇ ਵੇਲੇ ਇੱਕ ਔਰਤ ਉਸਦੀ ਦੁਕਾਨ ਵਿੱਚ ਆਈ। "ਉਹ ਜੁੱਤੀਆਂ ਦਾ ਜੋੜਾ ਬਹੁਤ
ਸੋਹਣਾ ਹੈ", ਉਸਨੇ ਕਿਹਾ। "ਉਸਦੀ ਕੀਮਤ ਕੀ ਹੈ?"
ਮੋਚੀ ਨੇ ਉਸਨੂੰ ਕੀਮਤ ਦੱਸੀ ਪਰ ਜਿੰਨੇ ਪੈਸੇ ਉਸਨੇ ਦੱਸੇ ਸਨ ਉਸ ਔਰਤ ਨੇ ਉਸਤੋਂ
ਦੁੱਗਣੇ ਪੈਸੇ ਮੋਚੀ ਨੂੰ ਦਿੱਤੇ।

Just then a woman came in to the shop. "Those shoes are gorgeous,"
she said. "How much are they?"
The shoemaker told her the price but she gave him twice the money
he had asked for.

ਹੁਣ ਮੋਚੀ ਕੋਲ਼ ਖਾਣ ਦਾ ਸਮਾਨ ਅਤੇ ਦੋ ਜੋੜੇ ਜੁੱਤੀਆਂ ਬਣਾਉਣ ਵਾਸਤੇ ਚਮੜਾ ਖਰੀਦਣ ਲਈ ਪੈਸੇ ਸਨ।

Now the shoemaker had enough money to buy food and some leather to make two pairs of shoes.

ਕਤਰ, ਕਤਰ! ਕਤਰ, ਕਤਰ!
ਉਸਨੇ ਚਾਰ ਜੁੱਤੀਆਂ ਬਨਾਉਨ ਲਈ ਚਮੜਾ ਕੱਟਿਆ।

Snip, snip! Snip, snip!
He cut out the shapes of four shoes.

ਉਸਨੇ ਤਿਆਰ ਕੀਤੇ ਚਮੜੇ ਨੂੰ ਸਵੇਰ ਨੂੰ ਸਿਉਨ
ਵਾਸਤੇ ਕੰਮ ਕਰਨ ਦੇ ਅੱਡੇ ਤੇ ਰੱਖ ਦਿੱਤਾ।

He left them on the workbench ready
to start sewing in the morning.

ਅਗਲੇ ਦਿਨ ਸਵੇਰੇ ਜਦੋਂ ਉਹ ਹੇਠਾਂ ਆਇਆ ਤਾਂ ਉਸਨੂੰ... ਦੋ ਬਹੁਤ ਸੋਹਣੇ ਜੁੱਤੀਆਂ ਦੇ ਜੋੜੇ ਮਿਲੇ।
"ਮੈਂ ਹੈਰਾਨ ਹਾਂ ਕਿ ਇਹ ਜੁੱਤੀਆਂ ਕਿਸਨੇ ਬਣਾਈਆਂ ਹਨ?" ਉਸਨੇ ਸੋਚਿਆ।
ਉਸੇ ਵੇਲੇ ਇੱਕ ਪਤੀ–ਪਤਨੀ ਦੁਕਾਨ ਵਿੱਚ ਆਏ। "ਉਹ ਜੁੱਤੀਆਂ ਦੇਖ," ਆਦਮੀ ਨੇ ਕਿਹਾ।
"ਇੱਕ ਜੋੜਾ ਤੁਹਾਡੇ ਵਾਸਤੇ ਅਤੇ ਇੱਕ ਮੇਰੇ ਵਾਸਤੇ ਹੈ। ਇਹ ਕਿੰਨੇ ਦੇ ਹਨ?" ਪਤਨੀ ਨੇ ਪੁੱਛਿਆ।
ਮੋਚੀ ਨੇ ਉਹਨਾਂ ਨੂੰ ਕੀਮਤ ਦੱਸੀ ਪਰ ਜਿੰਨੇ ਪੈਸੇ ਉਸਨੇ ਦੱਸੇ ਸਨ ਉਹਨਾਂ ਨੇ ਉਸਤੋਂ ਦੁੱਗਣੇ ਪੈਸੇ ਮੋਚੀ ਨੂੰ ਦਿੱਤੇ।

The next day, when he came down the stairs, he found... two beautiful pairs of shoes.
"I wonder who made these shoes?" he thought.
Just then a couple came in to the shop. "Look at those shoes," said the man.
"There is one pair for you and one pair for me. How much are they?" asked the woman.
The shoemaker told them the price, but they gave him twice the money he had asked for.

ਹੁਣ ਮੋਚੀ ਕੋਲ਼ ਖਾਣ ਦਾ ਹੋਰ ਸਮਾਨ ਅਤੇ ਚਾਰ ਜੋੜੇ ਜੁੱਤੀਆਂ ਬਣਾਉਣ ਵਾਸਤੇ ਚਮੜਾ ਖਰੀਦਣ ਲਈ ਪੈਸੇ ਸਨ।

Now the shoemaker had enough money to buy more food and some leather to make four pairs of shoes.

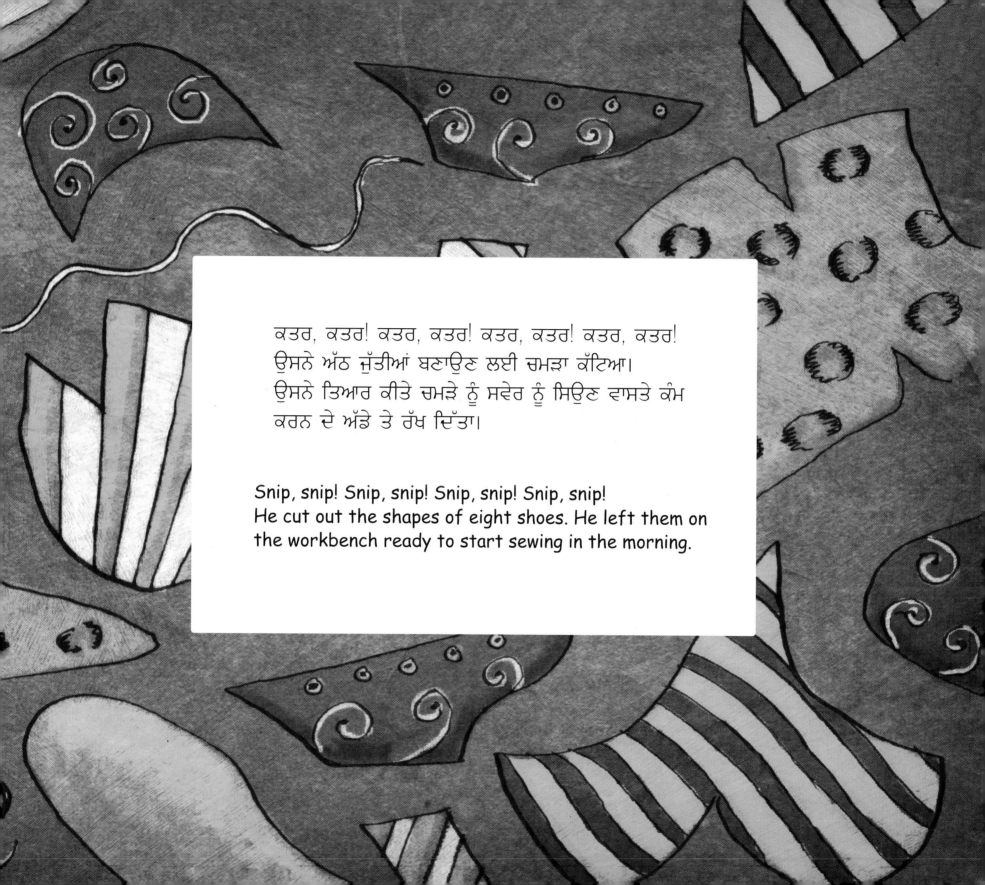

ਕਤਰ, ਕਤਰ! ਕਤਰ, ਕਤਰ! ਕਤਰ, ਕਤਰ! ਕਤਰ, ਕਤਰ!
ਉਸਨੇ ਅੱਠ ਜੁੱਤੀਆਂ ਬਨਾਉਣ ਲਈ ਚਮੜਾ ਕੱਟਿਆ।
ਉਸਨੇ ਤਿਆਰ ਕੀਤੇ ਚਮੜੇ ਨੂੰ ਸਵੇਰ ਨੂੰ ਸਿਉਣ ਵਾਸਤੇ ਕੰਮ
ਕਰਨ ਦੇ ਅੱਡੇ ਤੇ ਰੱਖ ਦਿੱਤਾ।

Snip, snip! Snip, snip! Snip, snip! Snip, snip!
He cut out the shapes of eight shoes. He left them on
the workbench ready to start sewing in the morning.

ਅਗਲੇ ਦਿਨ ਸਵੇਰੇ ਜਦੋਂ ਉਹ ਹੇਠਾਂ ਆਇਆ ਤਾਂ ਉਸਨੂੰ... ਚਾਰ ਬਹੁਤ ਸੋਹਣੇ ਜੁੱਤੀਆਂ ਦੇ ਜੋੜੇ ਮਿਲੇ।
"ਮੈਂ ਹੈਰਾਨ ਹਾਂ ਕਿ ਇਹ ਜੁੱਤੀਆਂ ਕਿਸਨੇ ਬਣਾਈਆਂ ਹਨ?" ਉਸਨੇ ਸੋਚਿਆ।
ਉਸੇ ਵੇਲੇ ਇੱਕ ਪਰਿਵਾਰ ਦੁਕਾਨ ਵਿੱਚ ਆਇਆ। "ਹੈਂ! ਉਹਨਾਂ ਜੁੱਤੀਆਂ ਨੂੰ ਦੇਖੋ!" ਮੁੰਡੇ ਨੇ ਕਿਹਾ।
"ਇੱਕ ਜੋੜਾ ਤੇਰੇ ਵਾਸਤੇ ਅਤੇ ਇੱਕ ਮੇਰੇ ਵਾਸਤੇ ਹੈ," ਕੁੜੀ ਨੇ ਕਿਹਾ।
"ਅਤੇ ਇੱਕ ਜੋੜਾ ਮੰਮੀ ਅਤੇ ਇੱਕ ਡੈਡੀ ਵਾਸਤੇ ਹੈ," ਮੁੰਡੇ ਨੇ ਕਿਹਾ।
"ਇਹ ਕਿੰਨੇ ਦੇ ਹਨ?" ਮੰਮੀ ਅਤੇ ਡੈਡੀ ਨੇ ਪੁੱਛਿਆ।
ਮੋਚੀ ਨੇ ਉਹਨਾਂ ਨੂੰ ਕੀਮਤ ਦੱਸੀ ਪਰ ਜਿੰਨੇ ਪੈਸੇ ਉਸਨੇ ਦੱਸੇ ਸਨ ਉਹਨਾਂ ਨੇ ਉਸਤੋਂ ਦੁੱਗਣੇ ਪੈਸੇ ਮੋਚੀ ਨੂੰ ਦਿੱਤੇ।

The next day when he came down the stairs he found… four beautiful pairs of shoes.
"I wonder who made these shoes?" he thought.
Just then a family came in to the shop.
"Wow! Look at those shoes!" said the boy.
"There is a pair for you and a pair for me," said the girl.
"And a pair for mum and a pair for dad," said the boy.
"How much are they?" asked the parents. The shoemaker told them the price, but they gave him twice the money he had asked for.

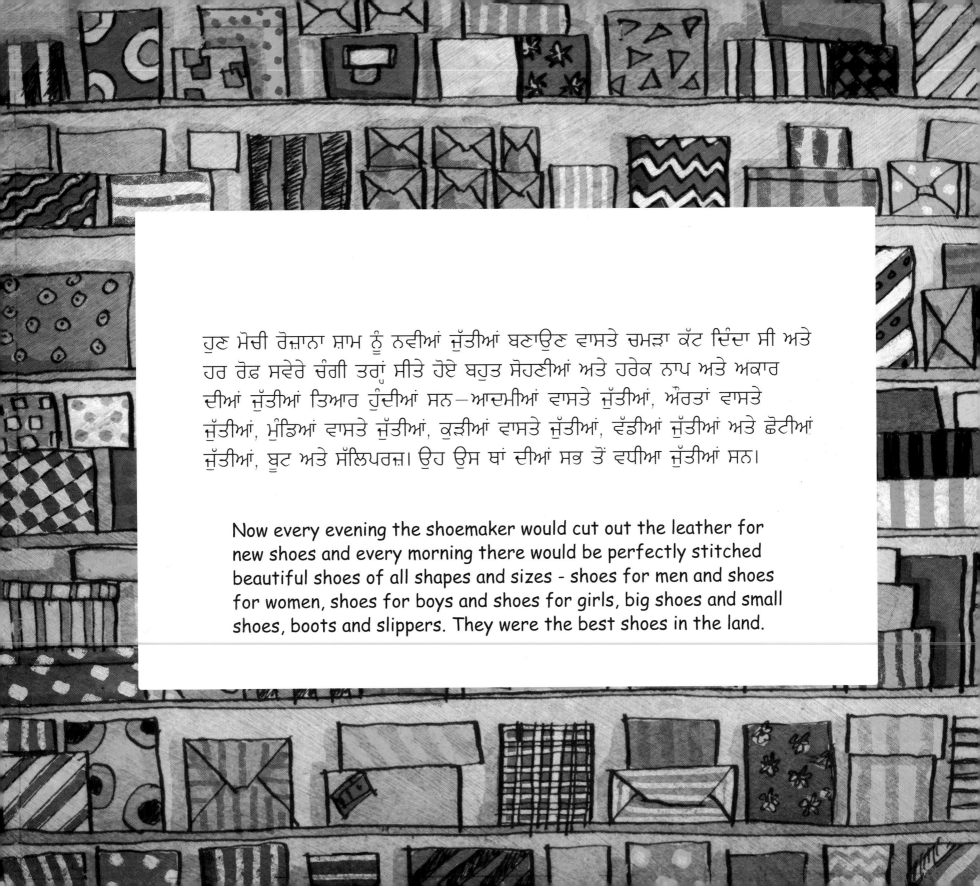

ਹੁਣ ਮੋਚੀ ਰੋਜ਼ਾਨਾ ਸ਼ਾਮ ਨੂੰ ਨਵੀਆਂ ਜੁੱਤੀਆਂ ਬਣਾਉਣ ਵਾਸਤੇ ਚਮੜਾ ਕੱਟ ਦਿੰਦਾ ਸੀ ਅਤੇ ਹਰ ਰੋਜ਼ ਸਵੇਰੇ ਚੰਗੀ ਤਰ੍ਹਾਂ ਸੀਤੇ ਹੋਏ ਬਹੁਤ ਸੋਹਣੀਆਂ ਅਤੇ ਹਰੇਕ ਨਾਪ ਅਤੇ ਅਕਾਰ ਦੀਆਂ ਜੁੱਤੀਆਂ ਤਿਆਰ ਹੁੰਦੀਆਂ ਸਨ—ਆਦਮੀਆਂ ਵਾਸਤੇ ਜੁੱਤੀਆਂ, ਔਰਤਾਂ ਵਾਸਤੇ ਜੁੱਤੀਆਂ, ਮੁੰਡਿਆਂ ਵਾਸਤੇ ਜੁੱਤੀਆਂ, ਕੁੜੀਆਂ ਵਾਸਤੇ ਜੁੱਤੀਆਂ, ਵੱਡੀਆਂ ਜੁੱਤੀਆਂ ਅਤੇ ਛੋਟੀਆਂ ਜੁੱਤੀਆਂ, ਬੂਟ ਅਤੇ ਸੱਲਿਪਰਜ਼। ਉਹ ਉਸ ਥਾਂ ਦੀਆਂ ਸਭ ਤੋਂ ਵਧੀਆ ਜੁੱਤੀਆਂ ਸਨ।

Now every evening the shoemaker would cut out the leather for new shoes and every morning there would be perfectly stitched beautiful shoes of all shapes and sizes - shoes for men and shoes for women, shoes for boys and shoes for girls, big shoes and small shoes, boots and slippers. They were the best shoes in the land.

ਜਿਵੇਂ ਜਿਵੇਂ ਰਾਤਾਂ ਲੰਮੀਆਂ ਅਤੇ ਠੰਡੀਆਂ ਹੋਣ ਲੱਗੀਆਂ, ਮੋਚੀ ਬੈਠ ਕੇ ਸੋਚਣ ਲੱਗਾ ਕਿ ਉਹ ਕੌਣ ਹੋ ਸਕਦਾ ਹੈ ਜੋ ਜੁੱਤੀਆਂ ਬਣਾ ਜਾਂਦਾ ਹੈ।

ਕਤਰ, ਕਤਰ! ਕਤਰ, ਕਤਰ! ਮੋਚੀ ਨੇ ਜੁੱਤੀਆਂ ਵਾਸਤੇ ਚਮੜਾ ਕੱਟਿਆ।

"ਮੈਨੂੰ ਪਤਾ ਹੈ," ਉਸਨੇ ਆਪਣੀ ਪਤਨੀ ਨੂੰ ਕਿਹਾ, "ਆਜਾ ਅੱਜ ਰਾਤ ਨੂੰ ਜਾਗਦੇ ਰਹੀਏ ਅਤੇ ਦੇੱਖੀਏ ਕਿ ਸਾਡੀਆਂ ਜੁੱਤੀਆਂ ਕੌਣ ਬਣਾਉਂਦਾ ਹੈ।" ਇਸ ਕਰਕੇ ਮੋਚੀ ਅਤੇ ਉਸਦੀ ਪਤਨੀ ਸ਼ੈਲਫ ਦੇ ਪਿੱਛੇ ਲੁਕ ਗਏ। ਅੱਧੀ ਰਾਤ ਵੇਲੇ ਦੋ ਬੋਨੇ ਆਦਮੀ ਆਏ।

As the nights became longer and colder the shoemaker sat and thought about who could be making the shoes.
Snip, snip! Snip, snip! The shoemaker cut out the leather for the shoes.
"I know," he said to his wife, "let's stay up and find out who is making our shoes." So the shoemaker and his wife hid behind the shelves.
On the stroke of midnight, two little men appeared.

ਉਹ ਮੋਚੀ ਦੇ ਕੰਮ ਦੇ ਅੱਡੇ ਤੇ ਬੈਠ ਗਏ।
ਸਵਿਸ਼, ਸਵਿਸ਼! ਉਹਨਾਂ ਨੇ ਜੁੱਤੀਆਂ ਸੀਤੀਆਂ।

They sat at the shoemaker's bench.
Swish, swish! They sewed.

ਠੱਕ, ਠੱਕ! ਉਹਨਾਂ ਨੇ ਹਠੌੜੀ ਚਲਾਈ। ਉਹਨਾਂ
ਦੀਆਂ ਛੋਟੀਆਂ ਛੋਟੀਆਂ ਉਂਗਲਿਆਂ ਇੰਨਾ ਤੇਜ਼ ਕੰਮ
ਕਰਦੀਆਂ ਸਨ ਕਿ ਮੋਚੀ ਨੂੰ ਆਪਣੀਆਂ ਅੱਖਾਂ ਤੇ
ਯਕੀਨ ਨਹੀਂ ਹੁੰਦਾ ਸੀ।

Tap, tap! They hammered in
the nails. Their little fingers
worked so fast that the
shoemaker could hardly
believe his eyes.

ਸਵਿਸ਼, ਸਵਿਸ਼! ਠੱਕ, ਠੱਕ! ਉਹ ਤਦ ਤੱਕ ਨਹੀਂ ਰੁਕੇ ਜਦ ਤੱਕ ਕਿ ਚਮੜੇ ਦੇ ਹਰੇਕ ਟੁਕੜੇ ਦੀ ਜੁੱਤੀ ਨਹੀਂ ਬਣ ਗਈ। ਫਿਰ ਉਹ ਛਲਾਂਗ ਮਾਰਕੇ ਦੌੜ ਗਏ।

Swish, swish! Tap, tap! They didn't stop until every piece of leather had been made into shoes. Then, they jumped down and ran away.

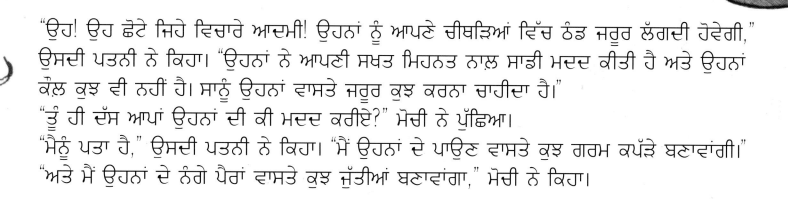

"ਉਹ! ਉਹ ਛੋਟੇ ਜਿਹੇ ਵਿਚਾਰੇ ਆਦਮੀ! ਉਹਨਾਂ ਨੂੰ ਆਪਣੇ ਚੀਥੜਿਆਂ ਵਿੱਚ ਠੰਡ ਜਰੂਰ ਲੱਗਦੀ ਹੋਵੇਗੀ,"
ਉਸਦੀ ਪਤਨੀ ਨੇ ਕਿਹਾ। "ਉਹਨਾਂ ਨੇ ਆਪਣੀ ਸਖਤ ਮਿਹਨਤ ਨਾਲ ਸਾਡੀ ਮਦਦ ਕੀਤੀ ਹੈ ਅਤੇ ਉਹਨਾਂ
ਕੋਲ ਕੁਝ ਵੀ ਨਹੀਂ ਹੈ। ਸਾਨੂੰ ਉਹਨਾਂ ਵਾਸਤੇ ਜਰੂਰ ਕੁਝ ਕਰਨਾ ਚਾਹੀਦਾ ਹੈ।"
"ਤੂੰ ਹੀ ਦੱਸ ਆਪਾਂ ਉਹਨਾਂ ਦੀ ਕੀ ਮਦਦ ਕਰੀਏ?" ਮੋਚੀ ਨੇ ਪੁੱਛਿਆ।
"ਮੈਨੂੰ ਪਤਾ ਹੈ," ਉਸਦੀ ਪਤਨੀ ਨੇ ਕਿਹਾ। "ਮੈਂ ਉਹਨਾਂ ਦੇ ਪਾਉਣ ਵਾਸਤੇ ਕੁਝ ਗਰਮ ਕਪੜੇ ਬਣਾਵਾਂਗੀ।"
"ਅਤੇ ਮੈਂ ਉਹਨਾਂ ਦੇ ਨੰਗੇ ਪੈਰਾਂ ਵਾਸਤੇ ਕੁਝ ਜੁੱਤੀਆਂ ਬਣਾਵਾਂਗਾ," ਮੋਚੀ ਨੇ ਕਿਹਾ।

"Oh, those poor little men! They must be so cold in those rags," said the wife.
"They have helped us with all their hard work and they have nothing.
We must do something for them."
"What do you think we should do?" asked the shoemaker.
"I know," said the wife. "I will make them some warm clothes to wear."
"And I will make them some shoes for their cold, bare feet," said the shoemaker.

ਅਗਲੇ ਦਿਨ ਸਵੇਰੇ ਮੋਚੀ ਅਤੇ ਉਸਦੀ ਪਤਨੀ ਨੇ ਦੁਕਾਨ ਨਹੀਂ ਖੋਲੀ।
ਉਹਨਾਂ ਨੇ ਸਾਰਾ ਦਿਨ ਕੰਮ ਕੀਤਾ ਪਰ ਉਹ ਕੰਮ ਜੁੱਤੀਆਂ ਬੇਚਣ ਦਾ ਨਹੀਂ ਸੀ।

The next morning the shoemaker and his wife didn't open the shop as usual. They spent the whole day working but it wasn't selling shoes.

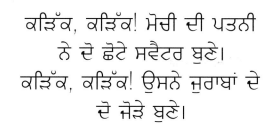

ਕੜਿੱਕ, ਕੜਿੱਕ! ਮੋਚੀ ਦੀ ਪਤਨੀ
ਨੇ ਦੋ ਛੋਟੇ ਸਵੈਟਰ ਬੁਣੇ।
ਕੜਿੱਕ, ਕੜਿੱਕ! ਉਸਨੇ ਜ਼ੁਰਾਬਾਂ ਦੇ
ਦੋ ਜੋੜੇ ਬੁਣੇ।

Clickety, click! The shoemaker's
wife knitted two small jumpers.
Clickety, click! She knitted two
pairs of woolly socks.

ਸਵਿਸ਼, ਸਵਿਸ਼! ਸਵਿਸ਼, ਸਵਿਸ਼!
ਉਸਨੇ ਗਰਮ ਪੈਂਟਾਂ ਦੇ ਦੋ ਜੋੜੇ ਸੀਤੇ।

Swish, swish! Swish, swish!
She sewed two pairs of warm trousers.

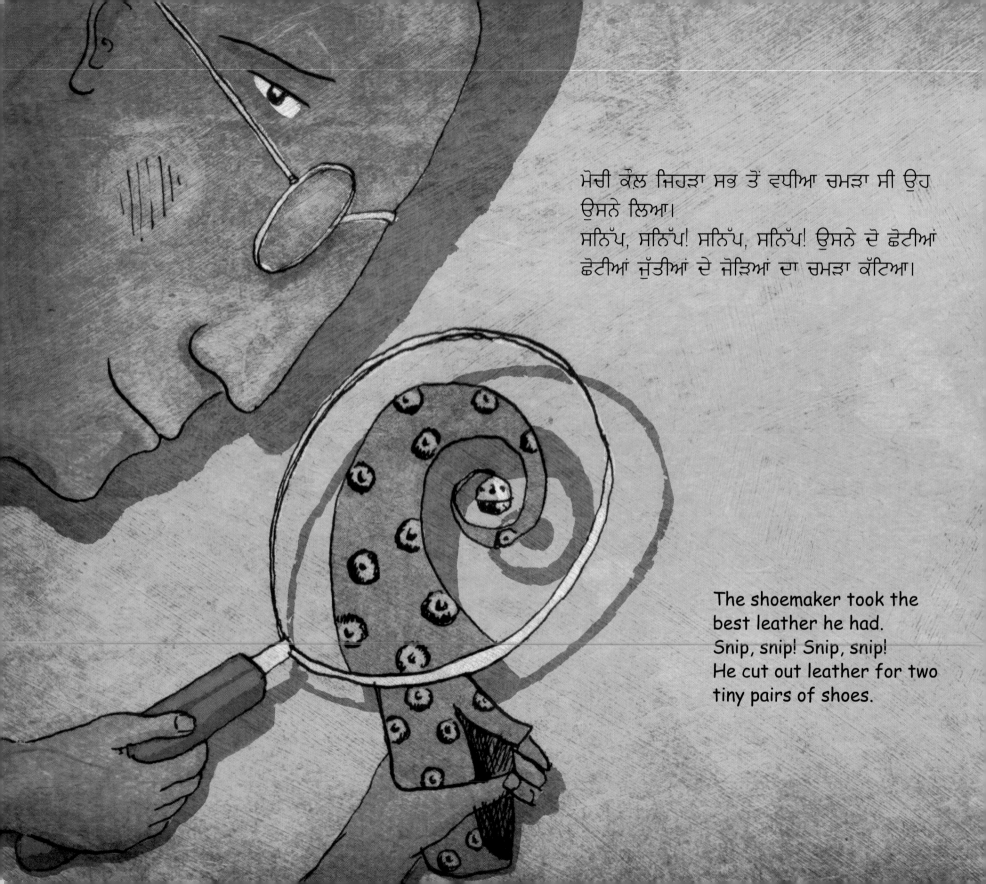

ਮੇਰੀ ਕੋਲ ਜਿਹੜਾ ਸਭ ਤੋਂ ਵਧੀਆ ਚਮੜਾ ਸੀ ਉਹ ਉਸਨੇ ਲਿਆ।
ਸਨਿੱਪ, ਸਨਿੱਪ! ਸਨਿੱਪ, ਸਨਿੱਪ! ਉਸਨੇ ਦੋ ਛੋਟੀਆਂ ਛੋਟੀਆਂ ਜੁੱਤੀਆਂ ਦੇ ਜੋੜਿਆਂ ਦਾ ਚਮੜਾ ਕੱਟਿਆ।

The shoemaker took the
best leather he had.
Snip, snip! Snip, snip!
He cut out leather for two
tiny pairs of shoes.

ਸਵਿੱਸ਼, ਸਵਿੱਸ਼! ਸਵਿੱਸ਼, ਸਵਿੱਸ਼!
ਉਸਨੇ ਚਾਰ ਛੋਟੀਆਂ ਜੁੱਤੀਆਂ ਸੀਤੀਆਂ।
ਠੱਕ, ਠੱਕ! ਠੱਕ, ਠੱਕ!
ਉਸਨੇ ਦੋਹਾਂ ਜੋੜਿਆਂ ਤੇ ਤਲਾ ਲਗਾਇਆ।
ਜਿੰਨੀਆਂ ਵੀ ਜੁੱਤੀਆਂ ਉਸਨੇ ਅੱਜ ਤੱਕ ਬਣਾਈਆਂ ਸਨ
ਇਹ ਜੁੱਤੀਆਂ ਉਹਨਾਂ ਸਭ ਤੋਂ ਵਧੀਆ ਸਨ।

Swish, swish! Swish, swish!
He stitched four small shoes.
Tap, tap! Tap, tap!
He hammered the soles onto each pair.
They were the best shoes he had ever made.

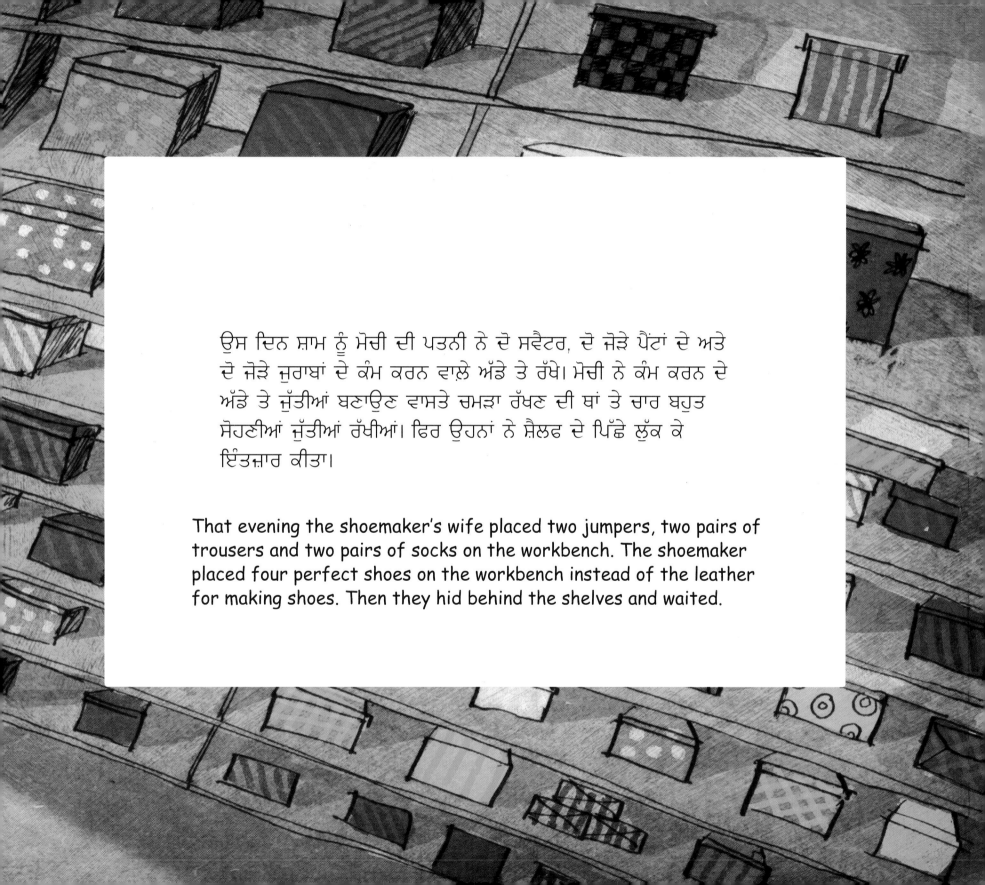

ਉਸ ਦਿਨ ਸ਼ਾਮ ਨੂੰ ਮੋਚੀ ਦੀ ਪਤਨੀ ਨੇ ਦੋ ਸਵੈਟਰ, ਦੋ ਜੋੜੇ ਪੈਂਟਾਂ ਦੇ ਅਤੇ ਦੋ ਜੋੜੇ ਜੁਰਾਬਾਂ ਦੇ ਕੰਮ ਕਰਨ ਵਾਲੇ ਅੱਡੇ ਤੇ ਰੱਖੇ। ਮੋਚੀ ਨੇ ਕੰਮ ਕਰਨ ਦੇ ਅੱਡੇ ਤੇ ਜੁੱਤੀਆਂ ਬਣਾਉਣ ਵਾਸਤੇ ਚਮੜਾ ਰੱਖਣ ਦੀ ਥਾਂ ਤੇ ਚਾਰ ਬਹੁਤ ਸੋਹਣੀਆਂ ਜੁੱਤੀਆਂ ਰੱਖੀਆਂ। ਫਿਰ ਉਹਨਾਂ ਨੇ ਸ਼ੈਲਫ ਦੇ ਪਿੱਛੇ ਲੁੱਕ ਕੇ ਇੰਤਜ਼ਾਰ ਕੀਤਾ।

That evening the shoemaker's wife placed two jumpers, two pairs of trousers and two pairs of socks on the workbench. The shoemaker placed four perfect shoes on the workbench instead of the leather for making shoes. Then they hid behind the shelves and waited.

ਅੱਧੀ ਰਾਤ ਨੂੰ ਦੋ ਬੋਨੇ ਆਏ ਜੋ ਕਿ ਕੰਮ ਕਰਨ ਵਾਸਤੇ ਤਿਆਰ ਸਨ। ਪਰ ਜਦੋਂ ਉਹਨਾਂ ਨੇ
ਕੱਪੜੇ ਦੇਖੇ ਤਾਂ ਉਹ ਰੁਕ ਕੇ ਉਹਨਾਂ ਨੂੰ ਦੇਖਣ ਲੱਗ ਪਏ। ਫਿਰ ਉਹਨਾਂ ਨੇ ਛੇਤੀ ਛੇਤੀ ਉਹ
ਕੱਪੜੇ ਪਾ ਲਏ।

On the stroke of midnight the two little men appeared ready for work.
But when they saw the clothes they stopped and stared.
Then they quickly put them on.

ਉਹ ਇੰਨੇ ਖ਼ੁਸ਼ ਹੋਏ ਕਿ ਉਹਨਾਂ ਨੇ ਤਾੜੀਆਂ ਵਜਾਈਆਂ—ਕਲੈਪ, ਕਲੈਪ!
ਉਹ ਇੰਨੇ ਖ਼ੁਸ਼ ਹੋਏ ਕਿ ਉਹਨਾਂ ਨੇ ਪੈਰਾਂ ਨਾਲ ਖਟ, ਖਟ ਕੀਤੀ—ਖਟ, ਖਟ!
ਉਹ ਦੁਕਾਨ ਵਿੱਚੋ ਨੱਚਦੇ ਨੱਚਦੇ ਦਰਵਾਜੇ ਵਿੱਚੋਂ ਬਾਹਰ ਚਲੇ ਗਏ।
ਅਤੇ ਉਹ ਕਿੱਥੇ ਚਲੇ ਗਏ, ਸਾਨੂੰ ਇਸ ਗੱਲ ਦਾ ਕਦੀ ਵੀ ਪਤਾ ਨਹੀਂ
ਚੱਲੇਗਾ।

They were so happy they clapped their hands - clap clap!
They were so happy they tapped their feet - tap tap!
They danced around the shop and out of the door.
And where they went we'll never know.

Key Words

English	Punjabi	English	Punjabi
elves	ਬੋਨੇ	sewing	ਸੀਉਣਾ
shoemaker	ਮੋਚੀ	making	ਬਨਾਉਣਾ
wife	ਪਤਨੀ	gorgeous	ਬਹੁਤ ਸੋਹਣੇ
shop	ਦੁਕਾਨ	price	ਮੁੱਲ
fashions	ਫੈਸ਼ਨ ਜਾਂ ਰਿਵਾਜ	money	ਪੈਸਾ
shoe	ਜੁੱਤੀ	cut out	ਕੱਟਿਆ
shoes	ਜੁੱਤੀਆਂ	stitch	ਤੋੱਪਾ
poor	ਗਰੀਬ	day	ਦਿਨ
leather	ਚਮੜਾ	morning	ਸਵੇਰ
pair	ਜੋੜਾ	evening	ਸ਼ਾਮ
workbench	ਕੰਮ ਕਰਨ ਦਾ ਅੱਡਾ	nights	ਰਾਤ

ਮੁੱਖ ਸ਼ਬਦ

midnight	ਅੱਧੀ ਰਾਤ	socks	ਜ਼ੁਰਾਬਾਂ
stroke	ਵੱਜਣ	clapped	ਤਾੜੀ ਬਜਾਉਣਾ
stay up	ਜਾਗਦੇ ਰਹਿਣਾ	tapped	ਖਟ ਖਟ
hammered	ਠੋਕਣਾ	danced	ਨੱਚਣਾ
rags	ਚੀਥੜੇ		
cold	ਠੰਡ		
bare	ਨੰਗਾ		
soles	ਤਲ਼ੇ		
knitted	ਬੁਣਨਾ		
jumper	ਸਵੈਟਰ		
trousers	ਪੈਂਟਾਂ		

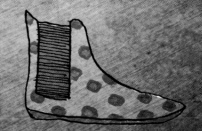

The books on this page have been Pen enabled.
Please touch the Pen to the left hand corner of the page for further information on language availability or visit www.mantralingua.com

TalkingPEN™

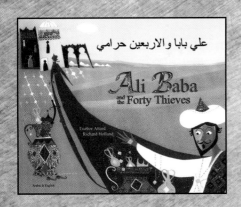
Ali Baba and the Forty Thieves

Неужели опять, Красная Шапочка!
Not Again, Red Riding Hood!
Kate Clynes & Louise Daykin

Ricitos de Oro y los tres ositos
Goldilocks and the Three Bears
Kate Clynes
Louise Daykin

LA PETITE POULE ROUGE ET LES GRAINS DE BLE
The Little Red Hen and the Grains of Wheat
L. R. Hen
Jago

LION FABLES
by JAN ORMEROD

三隻山羊加菲
The Three Billy Goats Gruff
Henriette Barkow
Illustrated by Richard Johnson

The Giant Turnip
Adapted by Henriette Barkow
Illustrated by Richard Johnson
Arabic & English

Beowulf
Adapted by Henriette Barkow
Illustrated by Alan Down

The Children of Lir
Dawn Casey & Diana Mayo

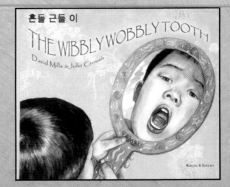
흔들 근들 이
THE WIBBLY WOBBLY TOOTH
David Mills & Julia Crouth